High School 101: Freshman Survival Guide

By the 2004-2005 Sophomores of
McIntosh High School
Peachtree City, Georgia
and their teacher
Dawn Burnette

G-ride Press
(an imprint of United Writers Press, Inc.)

G-Ride Press
An imprint of United Writers Press, Inc.
P.O. Box 326
Tucker, Georgia 30085-0326
1-866-857-4678

ISBN: 0-9760824-5-4 (trade paper)
ISBN-13: 978-0-9760824-5-3
Second Edition

Library of Congress Control Number: 2005926915

Printed in the United States of America by King Printing Company, Lowell, Massachusetts.

Cover design by Maggie Rector, Becky Atkinson, and Chris Wronski. Logo by Grant Stivers.

The first edition of *High School 101* was bound using a FASTBIND Elite Perfect Binding Machine by McIntosh students under the supervision of Jim Long, of ExactBind South. FASTBIND Elite is a trademark of the Maping Company.

This book was a project of the gifted/honors English program
at McIntosh High School, Peachtree City, Georgia.

The opinions and ideas in this book are those of the authors and other
quoted individuals, and do not necessarily reflect the views of McIntosh
High School or of any of its faculty or administration.

To order additional copies, please visit our website at
www.hs-101.com
or
send a check or money order
(payable to United Writers Press, Inc.) for
$14.95 + $3 shipping and handling
to
United Writers Press, Inc.
P.O. Box 326
Tucker, Georgia 30085

Special pricing for volume purchases and fund-raising is available.
For information, please call
1-866-857-4678

High School 101 is also available through
Amazon.com and booksellers nationwide.

Educators: For information on how to establish a publishing center
in your school or organization, please contact
United Writers Press and ask about
the Class Menagerie Program.

About the Project

The majority of "how to" books are written by adults. Why do they think they can advise kids about high school when they haven't been enrolled in years? Our philosophy for this book is that we understand today's freshman experience better than anyone else does because we have just lived through it!

As the authors of this book, we feel it is necessary to tell you our story. On the first day of school, we all stumbled into our new sophomore English class tired, worn, and depressed at the sudden and abrupt end of summer vacation. We all dreaded the outdated plays, long essays, and impossible tests often associated with gifted/honors English class. Many of us had been warned about the nature of our new teacher, Mrs. Burnette. However, try as they might, our elders had barely prepared us for the woman we'd meet at the bell's tone.

Our zany teacher talks about 150 words per minute and teaches material even faster. By the end of the first week, we had taken a test, written an essay, and critiqued our summer reading journals to the point of exhaustion. As the second week began, we were given the surprise of our lives: We were going to write a book!

Mrs. Burnette told us that she envisioned a survival guide for high school freshmen. Once she pitched the idea, we took over. At first we had a big pile of ideas. After we decided which topics the book should address, we researched, wrote, revised, and edited the content and organized it into chapters. We voted on chapter titles, layout, and cover design. We created our own ads and website, drew cartoons, took pictures, and conducted polls. We wrote business letters to bookstores, television personalities, newspapers, middle schools, and political leaders. We even participated in the binding of the books and went to state conferences to speak to teachers about our project.

After completing the bulk of the writing, we decided on a title for the book, chose G-Ride Press as the name of our publishing company, and created our own logo. A "g-ride" in our town refers to a golf cart, which is the main mode of transportation for most of us. In fact, McIntosh High School is the only high school campus in America with a golf cart parking lot—approximately 275 students drive golf carts to school each day.

Over the next few months, we critiqued, reviewed, criticized, and edited our way along. We worked like crazy on our Thursday "book days" during class and at our "book club" meetings before and after school. Otherwise, we went right along with our learning, never missing out on anything the curriculum had to offer. Yet, amidst Shakespeare, Aristotle, and Dante, we wrote our own masterpiece—one that we hope will shed some light on what's in store for upcoming freshmen.

We faced a few interesting obstacles along the way. Of course there were technological glitches—servers that went down at inopportune times, files that mysteriously disappeared, etc. Ironically, we also had a terrible time finishing the first draft of the organization and time management chapter. Perhaps the greatest challenge, however, was the fact that we were working with other students from different class periods but spent a total of only three hours in the same room with them at the same time! In spite of these problems, we were all determined to make the book a reality, so we overcame every obstacle that got in our way.

Your first year of high school is a critical one, and we hope our advice will help to ease this potentially rocky transition. Our goal was to make the content of the book universal enough to apply to freshmen at all high schools and in all parts of the country. We also tried to make the content informative yet entertaining at the same time. So read on and find out how to experience high school to the fullest!

Good luck,
Mrs. Burnette's 2004-2005 sophomores
(G-ride Press)

Special Thanks

Our class would like to thank the following groups and individuals for their support of and help with this project:

Carole Gilbert's AP Literature students
Donna Owen's gifted/honors freshmen
Fayette County Board of Education
First Presbyterian Church of Peachtree City
Georgia Association for Gifted Children
Georgia Council of Teachers of English
Her Majesty Queen Elizabeth II
JimLong@ExactBindSouth.Com
Judith Holbrook, proofreader
Kathy McAllister, parent
Kevin Belanger of Shepard Exposition Services
Kwik Kopy of Peachtree City
Lee Bailey, Fayette County BOE Network Administrator
McIntosh High School Computer Lab Paraprofessionals
McIntosh High School Joint Chiefs
McIntosh High School Media Center
Nancy Camp, County Office Duplicating
Omega Books of Peachtree City
Parent volunteers
Ronnie Ranes, web hosting
Susanne Routh and students
Tori Stivers, parent
Tracie Fleming, principal of McIntosh High School
Vally Sharpe and Jan Lowe, United Writers Press

Book Proceeds

Thank you for purchasing this book. We are using proceeds from its sale for two primary purposes. Some of the money is going back into our gifted/ honors English program to finance future projects. The rest of the funds will support charities chosen by the student authors. Proceeds from our first printing benefited the family of Ethan Peterson, a seven-year-old Utah boy with Neuroblastoma cancer. To make donations in memory of Ethan, you may visit *www.friendsofethan.com*.

Meet the Teacher

Dawn Burnette has taught English at McIntosh High School in Peachtree City, Georgia, since 1990. In addition to teaching students of all ability levels in grades 9-12, she has served as the English department chairman since 2002. Mrs. Burnette is the author and developer of Daily Grammar Practice (www.dgppublishing.com), a simple and effective method for helping students in first grade through college to understand, remember, and apply grammar concepts. Mrs. Burnette holds a bachelor's degree from Lenoir-Rhyne College and a master's degree from Georgia State University; she is a member of the National Council of Teachers of English and the Assembly for the Teaching of English Grammar; and she is a 2005 candidate for National Board Certification. In addition to publishing teaching materials, Mrs. Burnette has taught workshops for school systems and has presented at state and national conferences. Mrs. Burnette's latest publication is *Classroom Publishing 101: A Step-by-Step Guide* (www.dgppublishing.com). In April of 2005, Mrs. Burnette was honored as the Fayette County (GA) Teacher of the Year.

Authors

Aaron Arruda
Becky Atkinson
Rachel Barnette
Christopher Blackburn
Matt Bozone
Ben Brown
Matt Chambers
Kaci Clark*
Kelsey Clark
Thomas Cook
Matt Coppola*
Stephanie Cox
Carly Day
Carli Downs
Bilal Duckett
Jessica Everage
Morgan Flanders
Angelica Gentile*
Lauren Hedge
Morgan Hickson
Lauren Hook
Megan Houseman
Bryce Hughey
Jonathan Hung
Jorjeta Ilieva
Kelly Jackson
Katy Jensen
Natalie Kachadurian*+
Michael Kellim*
Michael LaCour
Jessica Lasseter+
Brigitte Lawhorn

Hannah Lee
Alba Lien
Eugenia Liu*
Matt Lovett
Patrick McAllister
Taylor Morris
Michelle Odakura*
Liliya Plotkina*+
Julian Prokay
Robin Prebor
Kelly Randolph
Racquel Ranes
Maggie Rector
Nicole Roddenbery
Elizabeth Rudd
Sarah Sowers
Lauren Spigner
Christina Statler
Janel Stitt
Grant Stivers*
Ellen Sturgill
Josh Thompson
Will Truex
Lyndsi Tufte
Crystal Weigle
Jane Welch
Craig Western
Reid White
Hannah Williams
James Wingo
Chris Wronski#
Michelle York

*writer/artist
+writer/photographer
#writer/graphic artist

Table of Contents

Table of Contents

Organization and Time Management

Note to Self:
Breathe at 2:30

"The great dividing line
between success and failure can
be expressed in five words:
'I did not have time!'"

-Franklin Field

Organization and Time Management

Are you the student who is constantly losing papers, digging through your messy locker, or forgetting homework? Do you try to get organized but then give up on the second day of school? If so, you probably saw the word "organization" in our chapter title and saved this section for last. Well, don't be afraid; we made this chapter just for you.

For many people, organization is not something we put much time into even though we should. However, disorganization is not the death sentence that it seems to be.

By following a few simple guidelines, you can be well on your way to being an organization guru. Even the smallest amount of time spent organizing makes a difference.

A good way to start is by using calendars, breaking things down, and making checklists. Take it from us: organization is a difficult concept to master. Nevertheless, it makes life a thousand times easier; it helps relieve stress, improve grades, and prevent those aggravating situations when teachers angrily tell you to organize your binders. So read on...we promise it's worth it!

> "Good order is the foundation of all good things."
>
> *Edmund Burke*

High school is a real balancing act!

Binders

Having organized binders is useful. To begin with, it is a lot easier to maintain schoolwork, homework, and projects if you keep them in a tidy binder. Organized binders also make your work easy to find. It is important to organize your binder at the beginning of the school year. If you take just a few minutes of your time to arrange a binder, you will be more organized throughout the school year.

We have several suggestions for starting and keeping an organized binder. First of all, throw out any papers that you will not use again. Save old, useful papers for future references by having a separate binder or folder at home. Such papers could include graded homework papers, old quizzes, tests, notes, handouts, and anything else that could help you later.

> **"Come with a plan to stay organized right away."**
> *Ms. Sullivan,*
> *World History Teacher*

Secondly, to save time, keep dividers in each binder to prevent papers from getting disorganized. Label the dividers into sections such as homework, class work, graded papers, and notes. Thus, you will be able to transition easily from one task to the next during class. Even if your teachers don't require dividers, using them is a successful way to stay organized.

Lockers

Lockers are beneficial for high school students because they lighten your load considerably. However, keeping them organized is another story. A good starting point for organizing your locker is to reduce the clutter. Try to get rid of the things you don't need. Also, go through all of your school papers and throw out anything that you won't use to study for future tests, quizzes, exams, or anything else you can imagine. After you discard all the clutter, hole punch the papers that you saved and put them in your binder. After all, if they are worth keeping, they are too important to risk losing.

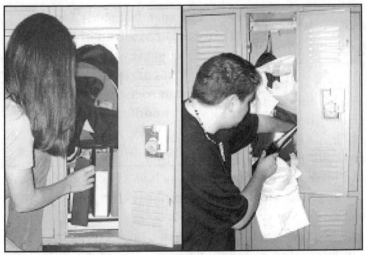

neat   messy

Locker organizers help you get to your classes on time and stay coordinated at school. Most office stores carry a wide variety of locker accessories including shelves, pencil holders, note pads, and much more. Of course, most items are magnetic. How convenient! Some lockers contain hooks or built in shelves. Take advantage of all the space given to you. Using lockers is optional, but if you have the space, why not use it?

Palm Pilot Replacement

Keeping an agenda is a crucial and low-cost step towards becoming organized. Agendas are commonly used for academic reminders such as homework, tests, quizzes, and projects. Not only can you use your agenda for school related items, but you can also use it for small things that tend to slip out of your mind such as taking out the trash, cleaning your room, recalling birthdays, or setting personal goals.

> "Use agendas; study for tests in advance instead of the night before; get involved in at least one extra-curricular activity and work harder than you did in middle school."
> *Mrs. Dykes,*
> *Spanish Teacher*

Once you get in the habit of using your planner, keep it in an easily accessible place. By employing it, you can possibly avoid receiving detentions or falling behind in class.

An agenda helps you follow your schedule and remember dates so that you don't forget any of your commitments.

Studying and Homework

In high school, the amount and difficulty of your homework will change according to your grade level and the type of classes you take. In your earlier school days, putting off assignments until the evening before they were due was all right—but it's not so simple in high school. Indeed, procrastinating in high school can lead to quite an unpleasant experience—especially when your grades drop as your workload increases. So how do you keep track of it all and not get bogged down in the mire of high school homework and projects?

First of all, try to use daylight hours to study and to complete homework. Studies prove that doing homework at night takes longer than it does before sunset—especially because at the end of the day, you're more interested in going to bed than in doing algebra. Also, try to prioritize your homework in order of difficulty and/or necessity. For example, if you have an A in world history and a C in Algebra II, do the homework for Algebra II first. By doing so, you can complete what is most necessary first. Furthermore, try to avoid outside distractions such as TV, radio, friends, or

> **"Study a little bit every night and do your homework."**
> *Mr. Jarrell,*
> *World History Teacher*

interesting pet behavior; these amusements detract from the attention you should be giving to your work and may end up directly affecting your grades. Instead, every time you get restless, get up and take a short break; then return to your homework.

It's a good idea to follow your class schedule when doing homework. For instance, if you have math second period and history first, do your history homework before your math. This way, if you goof up and forget to do an assignment due later in the day, you have several hours to catch up on it. (Note: Avoid making this mistake into a habit!) Occasionally, doing homework takes a lot of time—but the feeling of relief you get once you've finished is a wonderful reward. Additionally, when you finish homework early, the rest of your day is free.

> **"Do your homework; study more for tests than you did in middle school."**
> *Ms. Warren,*
> *Science Teacher*

Procrastination

Procrastination can make your school year miserable. If you procrastinate, it will be extremely difficult to survive your freshman year. Procrastination leads to the worst feelings you can possibly feel the day before the test: stress, disorganization, tension, inadequacy, depression, anger, and ultimately failure. It is very easy to get behind, and when that happens, life falls completely apart. Life doesn't have to be that way; if you did things in small steps and planned them out, life would be so much easier. There are many ways to prevent procrastination, and they are all easy.

One easy way to stay ahead of things and not procrastinate is to begin projects as soon as you receive them. Take it one day at a time, from beginning to end. Leaving a project or paper until the last minute

> **"Do not procrastinate; it causes unnecessary stress."**
> *Lauren, sophomore*

usually results in a disaster. Try to finish the paper ahead of time and leave touch ups for the last night. This reduces stress on your part and is less of a hassle. It is easy to say, "I have two months to do a project; I'll just work on it later." But usually things get put off, and before you know it, the project is due tomorrow.

There is also the solution of having a certain time set in the week to work on any kind of project. Try to use one of your free afternoons or any spare time. It's a consistent way of working on your project so you won't feel overwhelmed in the end.

Extra Time

Extra time is something everyone can use. Acquiring it, however, is easier said than done. Prioritizing is a good way to gain free time. Making a schedule of everything you need to accomplish will give you a clear picture of your time. Whether it is simply writing down your homework or making detailed lists, organization will get you extra time by helping you focus on what you have to do and making sure you finish everything.

Why do you want extra time? That question is not hard; anyone can think of a hundred things to do rather than do homework. On the other hand, we don't want you wasting your time doing such tedious acts as twirling your hair and chewing on pencils. You know what to do, so get it done. It is truly that simple.

Top 10 Ways to Waste Your Time

1. Read <u>War and Peace</u> in original Russian when you don't speak Russian.
2. See how many licks it takes to get to the center of a Tootsie Roll Pop.
3. Ride your grandpa's power wheelchair around the neighborhood.
4. Write a list of the top ten ways to waste your time.
5. Watch MTV.
6. Watch all 57 <u>Land Before Time</u> movies.
7. Try to understand women.
8. Learn to bend spoons with your mind.
9. Play calculator games.
10. Burn plastic army men with a magnifying glass.

Pointers for Time Management

> **There are 1,440 minutes in a day. Use them wisely.**

As you must or will know, high school students are some of the busiest people in the world. At this turning point in your life, balancing social and academic aspects is important. Though we are aware of the fact that we have said this repeatedly, again we utter the phrase: High school success depends on time and organization skills! Because we believe that these skills are extremely valuable, we have compiled a list of tips to help you manage your time and organize effectively:

☐ Begin the semester by filling in a master schedule. This would include all "fixed" events like soccer practice on Mondays and Thursdays, church on Wednesday afternoons, or band after school on Fridays. Then, analyze the "blanks" in your calendar and fill them as the days come along.

☐ Establish a regular time and place for study. This will save you time in the long run because you will have "programmed" your mind that "this is the time and place that I study."

☐ If you have a study hall during school, USE IT!!

☐ Use daylight hours to study whenever possible. It takes longer to study at night than it does in the daytime.

☐ Write down your daily assignments and weekly goals.

Being efficient in high school is directly connected to having good time management skills. Hopefully, after having read this chapter, you more clearly understand the importance and mechanics of organization. For even though time organization takes practice, it is definitely worth the effort in the end when you have all those wonderful extra hours left over to make abstract art or something equally as exciting.

Need More Info?

Covey, Sean. *The 7 Habits of Highly Effective Teens*. New York: Franklin, 1998. Covey takes organization a step further and includes life management skills. Although only one chapter is specifically dedicated to the topic of organization, the entire book is invaluable in its guidelines for effective teens. Sprinkled lightly over with humorous anecdotes, the seven habits mentioned in the title are clearly explored and explained.

Covey, Stephen, Roger Merrell, and Rebecca R. Merrell. *First Things First*. New York: Simon, 1994. This source illustrates how time management works in the day-to-day occurrences of one's life. It speaks particularly of how good time management can lead to good self-esteem, and later on to a position of leadership and possibly power. The book also stresses the importance of self-improvement through the practice of determination and motivation.

"Get Organized." 7 Jan. 2005 <http://homeworktips.about.com/library/weekly/aa010599.htm>. This website shows students how to manage their binders, homework, etc. It gives tips on ways to establish a schedule and stay on schedule. Tips for keeping up with agendas, schoolwork, grades, and binders are provided as well.

Organization/Time Management. 17 Jan. 2005 <http://
www.mccsc.edu/~mfisher/pride/Organization.htm>.
This website provides three useful links for time
management. Use them to expand and refresh your
knowledge of the subject.

Academic Success

Achieving It All

"The [academic] habits you learn in high school will help you in any career you choose."

-Debi Handy

Making the Grade

Now we know what you are probably thinking: "Academics…*sigh*," and that's not to say we don't agree with you. This is your first year in high school and you want the full experience. However, the fact remains that sooner or later we all need to know how to be academically successful. Why not get it done and over with now?

Although the broad topic of academics may seem a bit dull, the tips we have to offer may help you out on the long and sometimes frustrating journey of your freshman year. With our help, you'll find this topic is interesting and even entertaining! So get ready for the crucial ride into academic success.

Studying

Every student knows that studying is important; many, however, do not know how to study properly. For those who have not yet developed their own study techniques, here are some techniques that we have found effective:

* Making note cards: For some students, making note cards is one of the best ways to study. They are quick and easy to make and to use, and they are portable too. You can pull them out when you have a few spare minutes and quiz yourself. You can also separate the ones you're having trouble with and focus your efforts on them. It is a great way to use spare time.

* Reviewing notes: When studying for a test, remembering what is in your notes is crucial. Go over notes again and again until you know everything on them and feel secure about the subject. (Refer to page 24 for tips on note taking.) It is also great to reread your notes before class to review from the previous day. Go over your notes after class to become familiar with the new information. Make sure to ask your teacher questions about difficult concepts.

* Having a study buddy: Having a friend to study with is also a great way to learn. When you review and quiz someone over the material, it helps you to understand the material as well. Most people agree that you are more likely to remember what you are studying when you explain it to someone else. The drawback of this method is many times it becomes a

social hour. When you pick your study buddy, make sure it is someone who stays on task and will not distract you.

  * Do not cram for tests and exams. Although you can sometimes get away with cramming for quizzes, learning a whole group of sections in one sitting or at the last minute is not the way to go. You will not remember most of the information for the long term, which defeats the purpose of learning.

Academic Dishonesty

When people think about academic dishonesty, one word probably comes to mind: cheating. Well, cheating is a central part of it, but academic dishonesty consists of more than one thing. Academic dishonesty includes cheating and plagiarism, both controversial topics.

While both cheating and plagiarism were considered wrong in middle school, the consequences become much more severe in high school. Every school or system may have different rules and penalties for academic dishonesty, but in all cases, cheaters will be punished for their actions. Whether the student is given a zero, sent to the principal, or even suspended, teachers will never again trust those who have been caught cheating.

Plagiarism, the use of someone else's work without acknowledging that person, comes in several forms. Copying a quote without adding quotation marks is plagiarism.

Also, forgetting to cite or incorrectly citing a source indicates plagiarism. Even if you paraphrase information in your own words, you must cite the source. Although plagiarism can be unintentional, there is no excuse for not giving the author proper credit for his or her work.

Another form of academic dishonesty is cheating. Looking on someone else's paper during a test, copying another student's homework, letting someone copy your homework, using cheat sheets on tests and quizzes, and using papers from the Internet are all forms of cheating. (Many teachers are very strict about copying homework!) When grading papers, most teachers will be able to tell what is and what is not your work. Also, remember that in high school many teachers use different versions of the same test to prevent cheating.

Every student has been told a thousand times not to cheat, but in most schools, cheating occurs frequently. However, that does not make it right. The act of cheating is considered morally wrong and is never acceptable.

Cheating Tales

"The only test I ever cheated on was a spelling test in the 6th grade. I ended up failing the test anyway, and ever since then, I decided it wasn't worth it."

"I was cheating on this major history test one time. I mean, it's not like I hadn't done it before. But this time I got caught. I never thought it would happen to me, but it did. I got a zero on the test, and the teacher didn't trust me for the rest of the year. I would always have to go off to the other side of the room by myself whenever we took a test."

"I had a teacher a few years ago that assigned a research paper. Well as usual, I procrastinated and found out that I didn't have the time to do it. I found a copy of a similar report like the one I had to do. I thought she wouldn't notice, so I just copied it and turned it in. Well, I guess my teacher was smarter than me. She searched online, typing in some of my sentences, and found the paper on the Internet."

"In sixth grade I forgot to study for a geography quiz, so I decided to secretly use an atlas in my desk. When my teacher caught me, I tried to tell her that I thought we were allowed to use them; she didn't fall for it, and I felt rotten for the rest of the day."

Freshman Help Programs

Freshman year is when inexperienced students make most of their academic mistakes. Realizing this problem, schools are beginning to fight back; it is the obligation of the school to attempt to correct freshman failure rates, but even more so, it is the obligation of the students. Nationwide, schools are implementing programs to help freshmen get through the year without ruining their GPAs.

> **"Ninth grade is a transition year, so when it gets tough, hang in there!"**
>
> *Ms.Hubbard,*
> *Chorus Teacher*

To be helped at all, you must have a true desire to achieve. Intellect alone will not guarantee success; in fact, studies show that around 20 percent of all dropouts were academically gifted students. Many schools are learning that employing new technologies like computers, LCD projectors, and televisions in the learning environment increases the ability and desire to learn. Not all schools can implement this technology, but all teachers, parents, and students can work to create a good learning environment.

> **"Peer study groups are helpful if you stay focused. Sometimes hearing another person's explanation makes [the information] clearer."**
>
> *Debi Handy,*
> *Speech-Language Pathologist*

Hiring a tutor is another way to improve your chances of success. Tutors are very easy to find since most schools offer some sort of tutoring program. In addition to getting an actual tutor, parents, friends, and even teachers can be helpful. Teachers are often glad to help, partly because they look better if their students are succeeding, but mostly they take a genuine interest in the students' needs; not only can they help you in class, but they often provide study sessions before or after school. When you seek help, you will almost always understand the material better, increasing your potential for academic success.

"You'd think he'd be glad that I ate his homework. I mean, it didn't taste like anything better than a B-..."

Taking Good Notes

Taking detailed notes in class is an important skill that most students learn in high school. To take effective notes, you need to create your own personal formula. The first step in taking thorough notes in class is developing a standard method of abbreviations and making your notes legible. Try to copy words and phrases that are to the point; excess garbage will just clutter your notes and slow you down. Phrases like

> **"Colored highlighters help you form a visual picture of your notes."**
>
> *Debi Handy,*
> *Speech-Langugage Pathologist*

"this means," or "this person" or "because of this" usually signal that important information is coming. Always think before you start to write your notes and ask questions when you don't understand the material.

Use a large notebook so you have enough room to store as many papers as possible. Also, leave extra spaces as you are writing so you can add extra points later if necessary. If you need to choose between copying what the teacher says and what is written on the overhead or the board, stick with what is written because teachers will write the most essential information.

If your teacher does not give or dictate notes in an outline form, the textbook can be used to create an outlined version of the notes since most teachers stick to the book's general content. Keeping your notes in chronological order will help when you start to study. Studies show that taking notes helps you remember information even if you never go back and look at the notes again. Taking notes also keeps you focused on the reading or lecture. Taking good notes will be helpful in studying, and your grades will usually improve.

Top Ten Ways to Suck Up to Your Teacher

1. Use intellectual words and nod a lot.
2. Bring 14 sharpened #2 pencils to class.
3. Write an article about him for the school newspaper, or nominate him for teacher of the month.
4. Shout for joy whenever she gives you a test.
5. Always act like you know what's going on even though most of the time you have no idea.
6. Tell him how much fun school is.
7. Cover your binder with the mascot of the college that your teacher graduated from.
8. Bring her an apple...laptop.
9. When the teacher asks who stole the chalk, smile and point to the person next to you.
10. Hum "Hail to the Chief" whenever he enters the room.

Test Taking

Most people are not particularly fond of tests or quizzes. As a result, they do not score as well on their quiz or test as they would have hoped, and the amount of stress caused by their failure to study properly and by their low grade only makes them dislike tests and quizzes more.

> **"Doing your homework, studying hard, and trying not to fall asleep in class are the best ways to improve your grades."**
> *Mitchell, junior*

Simply studying more for each test or quiz without a clear idea of what you are doing only reinforces bad study habits. However, when you combine specific study techniques and test-taking strategies with a confident attitude toward tests and quizzes, not only will your grades improve, but the process of taking tests and quizzes will be much

more endurable if not comfortable.

One of the most important things to know about tests and quizzes is that no two tests or quizzes are the same! Likewise, the questions on tests and quizzes will be different as well. Now most people would dismiss this fact and say that it is the most obvious thing in the world, and they would be half right. People know that there are differences, but they fail to use this knowledge properly to improve their test-taking skills. Here are some quick pointers to get you into the correct mindset:

* Quizzes will focus on specifics while test questions will address broader topics.
* Any test questions that are specific will not be as hard as specific quiz questions.
* Read each question carefully; in multiple-choice questions, test makers anticipate possible wrong answers and put them as answer choices.
* Difficult questions might be answered in other questions later on.
* A partly false answer is a false answer, but a partly true answer is not always a true answer.
* Answer the easy matching questions first so you can use elimination to solve harder questions.
* Stay on topic and concentrate on the facts while writing an essay.
* There are three generic types of quizzes: "pop" quizzes, "vocabulary" style quizzes, and regular section review quizzes.
* Prepare for pop quizzes by reviewing your notes daily.

* Vocabulary-style quizzes are short quizzes that usually involve memorization of vocabulary words or term definitions; they should take 20 minutes or less to study for.
* Regular section review quizzes are mini-tests that cover specifics.

One of the best things you can do to personalize your test-taking strategy is to know the amount of application and memorization needed. An individual subject requires a certain amount of application—using knowledge in different situations—and a certain amount of memorization. Math, for example, is almost all application, while history and vocabulary are almost all memorization. By wasting your time practicing these abilities disproportionately to the amount required for a given subject, you will be very frustrated when it comes time to take the test or quiz.

> "Don't let your GPA drop during your freshman year because it makes it harder for your next three years."
> *Dr. Rawlings,*
> *Biology Teacher*

If you follow these general guidelines, tests and quizzes will no longer feel like arduous tasks but like predictable inconveniences. Even if you have great academic knowledge, no one reading your college transcript will think so if you do not have the invaluable skills to be a successful test and quiz taker.

Need More Info?

Berry, Marilyn. *Help Is on the Way for: Taking Notes.*
Sebastopol: Weekly Reader, 1985. This book
includes directions for writing notes, research
papers, and bibliographies for books, magazines,
and interviews. Also, it teaches how to write notes
for your paper as you go. Even if you have to write
notes quickly in class, you should rewrite the notes
at home to make studying easier.

Bobette, Brian. "Brain Quiz." 14 Oct. 2004 <http://
www.passionup.com/fun/fun4414.htm>. This site
explains the difference between being left-brained
and right-brained. A twenty-five-question test
determines your predominant side of your brain.
After calculating your score, the site explains
which subjects you are probably good at as well as
information to find the best ways for you to study
and learn.

Canavan, Peter. "How to Study." 3 Oct. 2004 <http://www.
how-to-study.com/>. This website offers ways to
study effectively, listen in class, and take notes.
However, there are no links to specifics. It tells
you how to improve your reading. Information on
creating index cards, writing papers, and keeping
track of your assignments is also included.

Covey, Sean. *The 7 Habits of Highly Effective Teens.* New
York: Simon & Schuster, 1998. This must-read is

a guide to becoming a strong, well-rounded, and ambitious student and adult led by strong principles. It offers tips on self-image, peer pressure, academic success, and more. It is divided into seven sections or habits that build upon each other and guide you through with "baby steps."

Fry, Ron. *Ace Any Test: 4th edition*. New York: Career, 2000. This guide gives methods for test taking such as paying attention and making a study schedule. It even offers a template for making a study schedule. It tells you different techniques for answering different types of questions. There are many other similar books in this series.

Fry, Ron. *Take Notes*. Hawthorne: Career, 1994. This book has very useful information for taking notes, including step-by-step instructions. The book is also divided into subsections to help you achieve each step. The information is easy to understand since it is well organized and very relevant.

Learning Strategies: Maximizing Your Academic Experience. Academic Skills Center. 5 Oct. 2004 <http://www.dartmouth.edu/~acskills/success>. This site includes sections on managing time, stress, and anxiety; reading textbooks; taking notes; and studying. Each section also includes helpful materials for self-improvement in the particular subject area.

Robinson, Adam. What Smart Students Know: Maximum
    Grades. Optimum Learning. Minimum Time.
    New York: Three Rivers, 1993. This book
    includes everything from reading comprehension
    to managing time. Unlike other similar books,
    it explains how to improve your academic skills
    and what most teachers look for in certain types
    of assignments. The author provides questions to
    use while reading so that you can better understand
    what you read.

"Ten Top Tips for Academic Success." 4 Oct. 2004 <http://
    www.sdc.uwo.ca/learning/tentt.html>. In this site,
    students can learn ten important tips about being
    academically successful. Topics include skills for
    organizing, studying, and testing as well as many
    more. Students that follow these tips will not only
    improve their grades but will also better understand
    the material.

TestTakingTips.com. 5 Oct. 2004 <http://www.
    testtakingtips.com/>. This site gives advice for
    taking tests, taking effective notes, and studying
    efficiently. Surprisingly, it even provides a sincere
    way to cram. It also provides information on
    specific types of test questions and recommends
    what to do before and after the test. It is easy to
    locate specific information because the site is simple.

Getting Involved

Being a Part of the Group

"It says a lot about a person's character when that person gives of himself to others."

-Sandy Perrin

Getting Involved

So you have entered the fast-paced world of high school and learned your schedule, but what do you do now? After-school activities are good ways to spend your afternoons. Meeting new people and doing fun activities is more fulfilling than watching TV all day.

> "Get involved in at least one sport; it gives the chance to exercise and stay in shape, and you can make new friends, too!"
> *Reid, sophomore*

Getting involved is also one of the major things colleges look for. Many after-school activities await you ranging from football to chess club. There is no reason not to get involved, so what are you waiting for?

Whatever your interests may be, your school probably has a club or group for you. If you are the academic type, you might enjoy such clubs as Academic Bowl, Science Olympiad, and Yearbook. For the more athletically inclined individuals, a school sports team may be right for you.

> "Join as many clubs as possible."
> *Hannah, sophomore*

There are also organizations such as Beta Club or Key Club for students who want to be involved in more community service related activities. Extracurricular activities not only provide you with a source of fun, but they also teach values and skills that can last a lifetime.

Options

Each activity has its own benefits and opportunities. For example, a sport rewards you physically by building strength and skill, and it also teaches you to work hard and persevere. If you are considering joining a sports team, do not be afraid to try new things. You never know what you are good at until you try it. Chances are  that your school will have a multitude of sports teams to choose from.

Likewise, service organizations like Beta Club or Key Club add character by teaching generosity, and the participants in the clubs help the community at the same time. Also, personal interest clubs can help you to explore different subjects of your choice. These clubs (which include language and political clubs) allow you to participate in activities concerning something that may interest you,

> **"You need to get involved in your freshman year. Do extracurricular activities and participate in things with other people."**
>
> *Ben,*
> *sophomore*

but not necessarily interest your friends. Personal interest activities usually do not consume too much of your time, and they provide you with opportunities to expand your knowledge in a particular area.

Poll

Which extracurricular activities are you involved in?

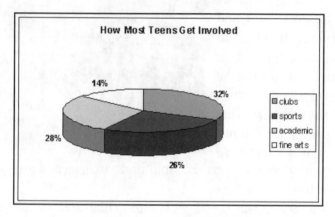

How Most Teens Get Involved

- clubs
- sports
- academic
- fine arts

14% | 32% | 28% | 26%

Choosing

Some research is required when trying to find a club that is right for you. Look into how often the club or team meets and how long the meetings generally last. Also, check to see if the activity requires time out of your weekend. Ask yourself how much time and effort you are willing to spend on being in the club or on the team. Do not try to join all the clubs in the school; it will be a disaster. Pick a few of your favorites and get involved.

College Benefits

After-school jobs are another option for teens; colleges constantly look for those who are dedicated and stable enough to hold a job during the school year. Another benefit of being involved is that it displays your dedication, well-roundedness, and ability to manage time wisely. College applications decorated with after-school participation credits gain more attention from the college admission representatives than do applications without them.

> **"Being involved in multiple things looks good on college applications, and you make many new friends."**
> *Anna, junior*

Meeting New People

What better way to meet new people than to join an extracurricular activity? Because students in the same clubs or organizations possess some of the same interests, it is only a matter of time before you make close friendships. Also, this is a good way to meet some of the upperclassmen you see around school. Most activities attract members from all grade levels, so it is possible to become friends with some of the older students outside of school. You may even develop an unexpected friendship with someone you barely knew before joining the activity.

Staying Busy

Staying busy during the school year is important. Although you should not enlist in too many activities, it is essential that you keep busy and avoid wasting time. Extracurricular activities are a great way to make your free time interesting, fun, and purposeful.

Top 10 Excuses for Not Participating in Extracurricular Activities

1. I left the stove on.
2. I'm too busy translating the dictionary into Mandarin Chinese.
3. I'm occupied reading a list of excuses for not participating in extracurricular activities.
4. I'm arranging my notebook paper by weight.
5. I'm finishing my earwax sculpture of Tom Cruise.
6. I'm trying to find a word that rhymes with orange.
7. Aliens have scheduled me for an abduction at two o'clock.
8. My cat is depressed, and I'm afraid I can't leave him alone.
9. My couch will miss me.
10. My personal trainer advises me to sit this one out.

Getting Overbooked

So you have decided that you want to get involved in extracurricular programs, but when should you stop joining? Overbooked schedules are a major problem for students nowadays. With so many clubs and teams to join, the possibilities are endless.

Problems occur when teenagers try to join every club possible, leaving no time for schoolwork. Studying and homework time should be your top priorities, as teachers give more tests, larger amounts of homework, and more complex projects than they did in middle school. If you don't leave time for schoolwork, your grades will begin to slip. Once you

> **"You need to find a balance between academics and extracurricular activities."**
>
> *Coach Stockdale,*
> *World History Teacher*

run out of time for studying, you become overbooked. Next, you must be able to dedicate yourself to the clubs you plan on joining. Clubs do not want a student who is unwilling to dedicate his or her own personal time to the club. If you join too many clubs, you cannot pay attention to all of them. Make sure you also set aside time to spend with your friends; this will provide you time to relax and socialize. Overall, one of the best ways to prevent a schedule overload is through careful planning of your day-to-day schedule and careful consideration of what activities and clubs that interest you the most.

With so many choices, it is hard to give advice, but choose wisely, for the person deeply involved in only one or two things is far better off than the person who is only slightly involved in everything.

Don't be too enthusiastic; choosing too many activities could impact your performance in all of them.

Don't be too enthusiastic; choosing too many activities could impact your performance in all of them.

Need More Info?

Beck, Sonya. "Extracurricular Activities." 15 July 2003. *College Prep-101*. 11 Oct. 2004 <http:// home. okstate.edu/homepages.nsf/toc/chp20_1>. An actively involved student at Oklahoma State University wrote this article based on her experience with extracurricular activities. This article lists steps on how to get involved and how to find the perfect activity. Also, it gives tips on reaching goals, staying involved, and remaining focused.

"Extracurricular Activities: Life Outside the Classroom." 2004. The College Board. 11 Oct. 2004 <http://www.collegeboard.com/article/0,3868,2-70-113,00.html>. This site addresses the fact that colleges pay attention to out-of-school activities, not just your grades. The College Board suggests that community service, volunteer work, or just getting a job is a good alternative to extracurricular activities. Also, College Board mentions that it's the quality and quantity of what you learned that counts to colleges.

"The Extracurricular Edge: Quality over Quantity." *College Board.com for Parents Home* Page. 12 Oct. 2004 <http://www.collegeboard.com/parents/article /0,3708,703-804-0-21282,00.html>. The article on this website emphasizes the importance of not getting overloaded by joining every club and activity you can. Colleges do not just look for how many clubs you join; they take note of your personal commitment to each club.

"Extracurricular Excitement." *Teens Health: Answers and Advice*. 4 Jan. 1995. <http://kidshealth.org/teen/school_jobs/school/involved_school.html>. This website is a great place to look up extracurricular activities that may be available at your school or in your community. The website is age appropriate for freshmen and gives examples of activities for all types of people. The site also has links to other helpful sites.

Investigating in Futures Homepage. 12 Oct. 2004 <http://www.plan4if.cslf.org/>. The information in the "Plan For College" section is very helpful for freshmen. There is information on which courses to choose in high school, guides for each year of high school, tips for how you can use your counselor as a valuable tool, and information on extracurricular activities.

Mitchell, Joyce Slayton. *Winning the Heart of the College Admissions Dean: An Expert's Advice for Getting into College*. California: Ten Speed, 2001. This book gives the most informative details on how to get involved with after-school activities. Also, the book gives real life situations that you may end up in. Ivy League school deans also voice their opinions on extracurricular activities and how you can find the activity that's right for you.

Personal
Well-Being

Me, Myself, and I

"If you do not conquer self, you will be
conquered by self."

-Napoleon Hill

Open the doors of a typical "story-book" high school, and what do you see? In the stereotypical world, you'll see teenage girls with perfect white smiles, football players escorting their cheerleader girlfriends to class, and as always, the classic nerd carrying too many books.

Whoa, reality check! The reality is that if you were to look beyond, deep into the darkest caverns of the students' hearts and souls, you could fill books and books with jaw-dropping stories of what really goes on in our world today.

Right beneath our very noses, students are dealing with mental and emotional stress, eating disorders, and substance abuse. Alarmingly, many are having suicidal thoughts or are depressed and using alcohol or drugs to escape the problems that torment their minds. Don't let what you find intimidate you. Open your mind and forget the "story-book" high school idea, and let yourself be educated on some of the toughest issues that teenagers face today.

> **"Don't be afraid to be different."**
>
> *Alex, junior*

Stress

Stress: Everyone has heard of it, but who really knows what stress is? Stress is the reaction of the body to anything that is surprising or unexpected. Being stressed has some very bad side effects, but don't let that cause you stress either. There are many ways to deal with stress in your life. First, however, you must understand the basic concepts.

Not all stress is bad; believe it or not, there is a "good stress," and everyone has experienced this type as well. "Good stress" is called positive stress. Say, for instance, that you are throwing a surprise party for your friend and are waiting for him or her to open the door so you can shout, "SURPRISE!" While waiting for that person to arrive, you are undergoing positive stress. Do not worry. Positive stress will not hurt you; it is good for the body. Think of it this way: If you went through life with everything planned and without surprises or twists, it would be very boring. Stress is like an alarm clock that goes off when something out of the ordinary happens.

Like all things in the universe, there is a light side and a dark side of stress. The wrong kind of stress can cause problems. "Bad stress" is called negative stress. It has many harmful effects to it. It can cause high blood pressure, high metabolism, depression, sleep loss, etc. There are many ways to deal with bad stress, such as reading a book, listening to music, hanging out with friends, screaming into a pillow, or just simply relaxing! Using the advice in the other chapters of this book will also help you reduce the stress of life in high school.

Depression/Suicide

Depression is not just "a bad hair day" or "the blues." It is a broad term that describes prolonged feelings of despair and hopelessness. Every part of your life is affected when you have depression; your thoughts become negative, and your behavior is careless. Depression is more than an attitude, though; it is a chemical imbalance in the brain. Small events, such as breaking a glass, seem worse when a person is depressed because he or she is hypersensitive to mood changes.

Affecting as many as one in eight teenagers, depression is more common than it appears. A variety of people can develop depression; however, it seems to be more common in girls. Researchers know that depression runs in families, and it is possible that inherited genes can increase the chance of developing it. The death of a family member or a friend, the social environment around you, and substance abuse can cause temporary depression.

What are the effects of depression? Long-term depression can cause weight gain or loss and can weaken your immune system. All aspects of your life begin to suffer: family, friends, work, school, sports, and community activities. Soon, everything feels like it is going to fall apart, and thoughts of suicide creep into your mind. Depression can cause indecision and dysfunction within every aspect of life (spiritual, mental, physical, and social).

What are some signs of depression? Since there are so many different kinds of depression, it is very hard to diagnose. Some things to look for include:

o A persistent sad or "empty" mood
o Unsubstantiated feelings of hopelessness and sadness
o Feelings of helplessness or worthlessness
o A pessimistic and/or guilty attitude
o Fatigue or loss of interest in ordinary activities
o Disturbances in eating and sleeping patterns
o Lack of energy
o Irritability, increased crying, anxiety, PTSD (post traumatic stress disorder), and panic attacks
o Nervous behavior, heavy breathing, or stomach aches when stressed
o A difficulty concentrating, remembering, or making decisions
o Thoughts of suicide; suicide plans or attempts
o Unrelenting physical symptoms or pains that do not respond to treatment
o Paranoia

Only a doctor or psychiatrist can diagnose depression, but if you or someone you know is experiencing some of these symptoms, seek help immediately.

Getting help is especially important if you or your friend is thinking about suicide. Depression can be treated with therapy and medications. If you are worried about a friend, ask straight out if he or she is depressed. Then, talk to a parent or trusted adult who will seek the necessary help for your friend.

Story from a High School Student

I moved to Georgia in fifth grade. It was a hard change, growing up and leaving everything I knew behind. I am not sure what started my depression—maybe the fact that I was overweight, lacked friends, and was experiencing a new environment or family problems. In about sixth grade I can remember having feelings of sadness. I used to tell my friends that I was going to kill myself and honestly thought about methods of how to do it. The ironic thing was that death was my biggest fear. I craved the change I feared the most, which led to a bigger state of confusion. Seventh grade was hard; a friend and my sister unmercifully teased me about my body, which did not help my self-esteem. One time, after being made fun of at a dance, I remember trying to make myself bleed in the school bathroom, with the help of a screw sticking out of the wall.

I did not realize my problem until I was taken to a psychiatrist. My mother, unaware of my developing depression, thought that recent family problems could be causing my mental anguish. There I was diagnosed with mild depression and put on Wellbutrin (a medication). I experienced many side effects, including vomiting and a lack of appetite. I lost about 15 pounds and skipped my period for six months. Often, my hands shook so badly I couldn't hold a pencil in the air without dropping it. Over the period of time when I was under the care of my psychiatrist, I was put on several medications, some combating the side effects of others. In the morning, I took ten pills, and at night I took two more. It was a stressful time in my life, and the medication seemed only to make my depression worse. During that time period, I often stared longingly at sharp objects and had thoughts of overdosing on my medication.

I had stopped seeing my psychiatrist and was taken off the medication, but things did not get better. Until this day, depression is still a part of my life, but it is not easily visible to the people around me. My behavior does not hint at my depression most of the time, yet I am plagued with thoughts of hopelessness, and there are days when I do not want to get out of bed. Much of the time I feel as though everything is a bad dream and I will wake up at any moment. I look around me and see nothing but despair.

My story does not have a happy ending or a miraculous cure, but it is important to know that depression can be treated and that treatment is successful most of the time. I did not write this to discourage you from receiving help for yourself or for a friend, but to inform you of what I went through and continue to go through. For a long time I was afraid to tell anyone about what I was going through, thinking that people would think I was making it all up, or that they would get scared about what I had to say. It was this fear that made my depression even worse. Through experience I have learned that it is important to share your feelings, and you should not be afraid of what people think. Nobody should have to go through anything like this, and even I, as someone who has not found relief, believe that a person can cope with depression through persistence and determination.

Self-injury

Self-injury is a wide and mostly unknown form of self-mutilation due to the fact that people want to forget it exists. Unfortunately it does exist everywhere. Self-injury is a silent epidemic in our society today and is a controversial topic.

Self-injury is when one inflicts harm upon oneself. There are varying degrees of harm, but all are dangerous. Cutting, burning, and bruising are examples of self-injury. Self-injury usually involves more than one of these techniques. Common household items, like safety pins and razor blades, are sometimes used.

Self-injury is a coping device for some people. Although most people make a connection between self-mutilation and suicide, the two do not always correspond. Self-mutilation is often used to externalize the pain people are feeling inside because the pain is too much to keep in. Many use it instead of resorting to suicide. If you or someone that you know cuts, you need to tell a trusted adult right away.

Even the most unlikely of people can self-injure themselves. If you fear that someone you care about is injuring himself, note scars or cuts on his arms and look for sharp objects. Again, tell an adult if you feel that your friend may have a problem with self-mutilation.

It's important to understand just how dangerous self-mutilation is. Not everyone does it for the same reasons, but everyone who does it is putting his health at risk. Help is available for self-injury, and with time and patience a person can overcome it.

Story from a High School Student

Depression was always a part of my life, and I learned to live with it. All throughout middle school, I was the loner, the typical stereotype of a depressed person. I had few friends, I was the geek, and no one wanted to hang around me. At the end of my eighth grade year, I began cutting. I even resorted to burning myself with a lighter. It was a hard summer because I stayed in my house the entire time.

When I started high school, I was hoping for a change. At first nothing happened because I wouldn't let it. I didn't want to put myself out there because of the possibility of failure. I had such extreme anxiety over every little thing; I would only do what I knew I would be good at. Participating in debate, I was able to alleviate some of my depression, but it was still there.

Finally, in November of my freshman year, I hit rock bottom. I even attempted suicide and was sent to a mental hospital for five days. Coming back after that week was uncomfortable, but I was drastically changed. Depression, as ominous as it feels, can go away. I am an example of this; I went from rock bottom to basking in the sun.

Substance Abuse

Substance abuse, also known as chemical abuse, is the overindulgence in and dependence on an addictive substance. Commonly abused substances are alcohol, marijuana, cocaine, speed, and even simple household items. Substance abuse is a serious problem that affects an alarmingly large and constantly rising number of teens.

One of the most commonly abused substances is marijuana. To some people, getting high may seem harmless; but while under the influence, people often do things that they would not usually do. Studies have shown that teenagers are five times more likely to have sex while high on marijuana than when they aren't. Difficulties with potentially dangerous tasks, such as driving, may also arise.

If you or anyone you know has a problem with drugs or alcohol, there are several places you can go. At freevibe. com and samhsa.gov, you can find information on drugs and their effects. You can also call the National Substance Abuse Hotline at 1-800-DRUG-HELP or the National Drug Hotline at 1-800-662-4357 for confidential help. The best thing you can do is to talk to a parent, teacher, or counselor. To state the obvious, they have been your age before and can help with any problems you are facing.

Eating Disorders

As students face challenges and try to maintain control of their lives, some begin to develop eating disorders. The two most common eating disorders are anorexia and bulimia. About one in every one hundred 16- to-18-year-olds has anorexia nervosa; bulimia is even more common. Eating disorders are most common in teenage girls, but they also affect teenage boys.

> "As long as you're happy with yourself, there is no need to change."
>
> *Lisa, sophomore*

People with anorexia starve themselves, avoid high calorie foods, and exercise constantly. Those with bulimia eat huge amounts of food and later throw it up.

The media is a huge influence on today's younger generation. Teenage minds are bombarded with images of unnaturally perfect figures of models and movie stars. Top models are 5'9" to 6' and weigh 110-118 pounds, while the average woman is 5'4" and weighs 142 pounds. Every young girl wants to be told that she is beautiful, and in the back of girls' minds are memories of people telling them that it is what's inside that counts and that everyone is beautiful in their own way.

Children, primarily girls, are developing an obsession with body weight at the mere ages of 10 and 11 years old. Eating disorders are most common in societies where it is desirable to be slim, and America is not alone in having populations with high percentages of people with eating disorders. A survey taken of 200,000 teens from the United

Kingdom found that 60 percent of girls think they ought to lose weight, while statistics prove that only 10 percent of these girls are actually overweight.

Many wonder why people have anorexia or bulimia. It is a common myth that anorexics are not hungry. The truth is that anorexics are always hungry; by being hungry, they gain a sense of control over their otherwise out-of-control lives. While dieting and exercising right are fine, our obsessions with faultless bodies along with low self-esteem, troubled relationships, and sexual or emotional abuse can lead to eating disorders. It is important that sufferers of an eating disorder and their families realize how very dangerous eating disorders can be. Of all mental illnesses, anorexia has the highest mortality rate. Anorexics are quick to feel cold and get sick, are often grumpy, and have a hard time concentrating because they are always hungry.

The loved ones of the victims must realize the importance of treatment. The victims often believe nothing is wrong with them, so the condition may go undetected until it is too late. If you suspect that you or someone you know may have an eating disorder, it might be helpful to know how to recognize the warning signs, and what you can do.

Warning signs include deliberate self-starvation and weight loss, refusal to eat, denial of hunger, and a self-perception of being fat when in reality the individual is much too thin. Treatment is crucial. People with eating disorders will be quick to say there is nothing wrong with them, but it is important that their families and friends do not give into their denial and that help be sought immediately.

Eating disorders are a serious problem, but it is possible to prevent eating disorders in yourself and others. Share the knowledge you have gained about eating disorders with the people around you.

Daydreamer Diagnosis

Have you found yourself thinking about the weekend in the middle of math class? Are you hyperactive? Do people call you a "bundle of energy" or just "unique"? If so, stop before diagnosing yourself with ADD.

Attention Deficit Disorder is one of the most widely over-diagnosed conditions in the United States. Many other conditions exist for which ADD can be mistaken: dyslexia, autism, bipolar disorder, schizophrenia, right-brained thinking, stress, depression, and life in the twenty-first century just to name a few. It is good to know the facts without the fiction and to create a clear view of what is ADD and what is simply normal life.

True Attention Deficit Disorder is caused by a chemical imbalance in the part of the brain that controls the attention span. There are three main characteristics associated with the actual neurological condition: impulsivity, distractibility, and hyperactivity. Impulsiveness refers to thinking and acting almost simultaneously. For example, someone is dared to shave his eyebrows for five dollars and without hesitation grabs a razor and goes at it. Different variations of impulsivity can be present; however, distractibility must also be present for ADD to exist. Distractibility is the lack of ability to focus at any given time. However, people with true ADD also have the ability to hyper-focus on something of interest. When someone with ADD finds something interesting, he or she typically excels at it and does so with amazing accuracy. Hyperactivity can also be present in a person with ADD; however, it is not necessary. Some people, especially girls, with ADD are extremely calm and pensive.

You can have some or all of these conditions without actually having ADD. In order to be diagnosed with ADD, you must have had these symptoms before age seven. Symptoms that begin to show up at a later age are either due to another disorder, such as depression, or are just a product of the stresses of high school. So, be careful before jumping the gun with a diagnosis. Take your time and get all the facts before you pinpoint a specific disorder. Because of the usually busy nature of today's world, it may be that you have too much on your mind and are not concentrating as well as you normally could. Every teenager has occasional ADD symptoms; very few teenagers can actually focus all day every day. We all have our ups and downs; they are a part of high school, and they are completely normal. Ask your doctor or talk to a counselor if you suspect you are suffering from ADD or any of the other conditions mentioned. Consulting random internet tests is not a good idea; they are not entirely dependable and are rarely written by experts on the subject.

Regardless of whether or not you are diagnosed with ADD, there are ways to combat your daydreaming tendencies by developing your own coping skills to subdue them. Despite the diagnosis, it is comforting to know there is no such thing as "normal."

Hotline Numbers

Suicide
Hope Line Network
1-800-SUICIDE (800-784-2433)
Trained volunteers and professional counselors are there to listen.

Eating Disorders
National Eating Disorder Referral and Information Center
858-481-1515
An international organization to help prevent and inform others about eating disorders

National Eating Disorders Association
1-800-931-2237
An international organization to help those with eating disorders

Anorexia Nervosa and Associate Disorders (ANAD)
847-831-3438
Referrals to treatment and information about anorexia nervosa and other eating disorders

Overeater's Anonymous
505-891-4320
Referrals and information about overeating

Massachusetts Eating Disorder Association, Inc. Helpline
617-558-1881
Staffed by trained/supervised individuals that will talk about eating disorders
Monday-Friday (9:30-5:00 p.m.)
Wednesday until 8:00 p.m.

Bulimia and Self-Help Hotline
314-588-1683
24 hour-a-day crisis line

Mental Health
1-800-THERAPIST Network
1-800-THERAPIST (1-800-843-7274)
International mental health referral service

The National Mental Health Association Information Center
1-800-969-NMHA (1-800-969-6642)
Will help you find community mental health services and self-help groups

Panic Disorder Information Line
1-800-64-PANIC (1-800-647-2642)
Provides written information and referrals on panicking and panic disorders

Abuse
VOICES in Action
1-800-7-VOICE-8
An international organization to provide assistance to survivors of incest and child sexual abuse

Rape, Abuse, and Incest National Network (RAINN)
1-800-656-HOPE
Provides service for survivors of sexual assault who cannot reach a rape crisis center through local telephone calls. Operates 24 hours a day.

National Domestic Violence Hotline
1-800-799-SAFE
For victims of domestic violence and their family and friends
Child-Help USA
1-800-4-A-CHILD
National child abuse hotline offering crisis counseling for children or adult survivors 24 hours a day

Sexual Assault Crisis Line
1-800-643-6250
A national 24-hour hotline that can provide support

Self-injury Help
1-800-DONT CUT
Information and referrals about self-injury

Drugs/Alcohol
Alcohol and Drug Hotline
1-800-821-4357
Treatment centers and AA support groups

Need More Info?

"Beat Stress." *Stress Management*. 29 Oct. 2004 http://www.
    mindtools.com/smpage.html. This site focuses on
    ways to deal with stress. It lists twelve essential skills
    to manage stress. The site contains a test to see which
    of the skills will be most helpful to you. It also gives
    you relaxation techniques and lists stress-reducing
    establishments. Multiple articles, directories, and links
    are given throughout the site.

Clark, Melody. *When No One Knows Your Pain*. 1997.
    Meadow Lark Press. 6 Oct. 2004 — http://suicidal.
    com. This site relates directly to how a suicidal/
    depressed person is feeling. The author, Melody, talks
    directly to you and practically gets inside your mind. It
    has links to crisis centers, hot line numbers to call, and
    clinics you can go to for help.

Kirberger, Kimberley. *No Body's Perfect*. New York:
    Scholastic, 2003. This book will help you accept
    yourself for who you are. It will help you deconstruct
    the negative images that have been placed on you and
    rebuild your self image with a more confident one. This
    book teaches you how to celebrate yourself, learn from
    your mistakes, and do things for yourself.

Lebelle, Nick. *Focus Adolescent Services: Self-Injury*. 2000.
    Focus Adolescent Services. 13 Oct 2004 <http://www.
    focusas.com/SelfInjury.html>. This site provides
    you with definitions of what self-injury is and why

teenagers do it. It provides parents with a resource to better understand and find help for teens. Lebelle explains that self-injury is a coping device. Links on this site lead you to more specific areas of self-injury.

Miller, Gene. "Dangerous Rituals of Belonging." *Teen Speak* 2 Feb. 2005 <http://www.teenspeaknews.com /issue5/articles/rituals.html>. This article focuses on hazing and gives the readers direct examples of why it is wrong. This article is also useful because of the large quantity of examples and support for the topic. The writer uses references if the reader wants more information.

Peele, Stanton. "All or Nothing: The Extremes of Alcoholism." Sept. 1996. *Psychology Today*. 5 Oct. 2004 <http://health.yahoo.com/health/centers/ addiction/1058.html>. This website is about alcohol and alcoholism. It has a wealth of random facts such as how much is spent yearly on advertising, percentage of people consuming alcohol per year, and the drinking restrictions in other countries. Also, it lists different ways to recover from alcoholism including doctor's help.

TeensHealth: Answers and Advice. 10 Oct. 2004 <http:// kidshealth.org/teen/your_mind/feeling_sad/ depression.html>. This site goes in-depth about what causes depression, types of depression, and symptoms and is made for teenagers. Ways of getting help for yourself or for a friend are included along with many reasons why it is important to get help immediately.

Peer Pressure

5

Read This...You Know You Want To!

"It's just better to be yourself than try to be some version of what you think the other person wants."

-Matt Damon

Peer pressure: It's everywhere…isn't it? It's at parties, at work, at school, in public places, in the media, and even in private places. At some point or another, every teen is going to encounter something that makes him or her feel uncomfortable. Ranging anywhere from profanity to stealing to sex to drugs, it's going to happen.

Pressure

When someone pressures you to do something, ask yourself a few questions: "Do I feel comfortable? Could this get me in trouble? Would I possibly hurt anyone physically or emotionally? Will a higher authority disapprove?" The safest choice is to bail out if any of the answers are yes. It may not be the easiest or "coolest" choice to make in the minds of your friends, but avoiding a situation that you may regret will pay off in the end. Stick to your own personal morals and values, and you'll do just fine.

> "Something that seems like fun now may not be so much fun when you're still paying the consequences years from now."
>
> *Jessica, junior*

At times, a person who wants to belong to a specific group will change the way he or she looks and acts just to "fit in." Acceptance in some groups might mean dressing a certain way, smoking, drinking, or participating in harmful activities that can make you feel uncomfortable. You shouldn't have to change who you are to fit into a group. In the end, you are only going to lose your individuality or your self-respect.

Poll

Have you ever been pressured into doing something that you didn't want to do?
Yes, and I felt bad afterwards- 39%
Yes, but it was something positive - 42%
No- 14%
I don't think so- 5%

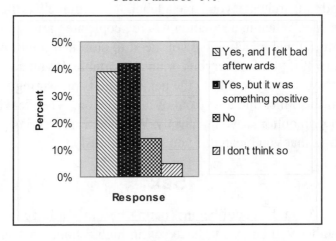

Alcohol and Drugs

In the transition from child to adult, teens do a lot of experimenting. Most parties involve peer pressure, so having an excuse to say "no" beforehand is a good idea. Many people become addicted to alcohol, drugs, or tobacco on the first try, and smoking and drinking are a huge part of the peer pressure equation every day. More and more teens are being pressured into smoking or drinking. As you already may know, high school students tend to put labels

> **"Just get away from people who pressure you."**
> *Jeff, sophomore*

on people; even if you try pot only once, you could be labeled a "stoner." Labeling could happen even if you are a good kid; and once you have a label, it is extremely difficult to shake. When in a situation where people are participating in questionable activities, you need to stop and think. Ask yourself if you feel nervous or uncomfortable. If you do feel uneasy, then try to talk to the person who is pressuring you, or if this fails, find a way out of the situation. When leaving is not an option, say "no" firmly. Whoever is pressuring you knows that you mean it if you say it seriously.

Sex

As high school begins, dating becomes a huge issue. Whether you choose to have sex in high school, wait until you are older and more mature, or plan to wait until you are married, sex should be your decision. We're not here to lecture anyone about how sex is bad or dirty, or how it will make you a bad person if you are curious about it. Rather, we are here to talk about uncomfortable situations that you may encounter with emotional relationships.

Boyfriends and girlfriends may seem very important to you in high school, but having sex with your partner will not make your relationship any more meaningful.

> **"Think about the consequences of your actions; see if they're good or bad."**
> *Katie, senior*

You may really like one person today and be disgusted by that same person tomorrow. Although saying no may anger, upset, or even embarrass your partner, it is important to make your point clear and continue to follow through with that decision. Sex is not a band-aid, a right of passage, or a joke. It is challenging enough to balance grades, sports, clubs, and friends; adding sexual partners and problems such as pregnancy and STDs just complicates matters more.

If you ever feel like you are being pressured into sex or are uncomfortable with any situation concerning sex, there are many groups and organizations, such as the PSI (Postponing Sexual Involvement) group, full of young people and teenagers who feel the same way. Organizations online such as www.abstinencebetterchoice.com can be accessed from anywhere across the country. Offering teens a guiding light through unwanted sexual encounters, these organizations can be very helpful for those considering abstaining from sexual activity until marriage.

Sex is a difficult subject matter, so it should not be taken lightly. Consequences are a part of peer pressure and can lead to many difficult problems. Whatever decision you may make about sex in high school or even into college and beyond, make sure it is your own educated decision.

Stealing

Stealing is also one of the many things people can be pressured into doing. Shrugging it off is not going to make the situation vanish. Some teenagers who steal aren't even planning on it in the first place; they see the opportunity and go for it. Some kids who steal do it even though they can afford to purchase the item. They do it for fun, or for the rush they get from getting away with it.

Stealing even small things will lead to larger and more dangerous crimes. Some of the most infamous criminals started by stealing other kids' lunches every day, or by taking something small like a pair of earrings. Walking out of any store with something you haven't paid for could leave you sitting in a security room in the local mall's basement, waiting for your parents to come and pick you up, or even worse, in a jail cell.

Friends

Friends can be right there to catch your fall if you should ever lose your way, but sometimes they can be the source of all your frustrations. Statistics show that young men and women are pressured into drinking, doing drugs, smoking, and having sex by their closest

> **"My real friends actually pressure me to stay out of trouble rather than do things that are illegal or immoral."**
> *Alan, senior*

peers and friends. Sometimes, if your close group of friends has one member who takes the first leap into a pit of no return, everyone feels the need to jump in head first after him to keep up with the changing times and to be accepted by the crowd. The ever-present need for acceptance often fuels first sexual, alcohol-related, and drug-related experiences.

Poll

Who pressures you the most?
Friends- 68%
Family- 13%
Role model- 1%
Celebrity- 1%
Other- 17%

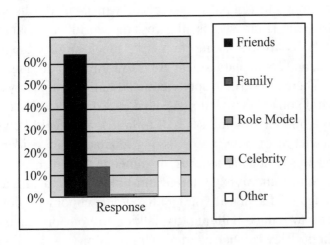

Bullying

Our society had made hazing and bullying acceptable until victims started to retaliate, as is the case in the Columbine High School shooting and others. There are many reasons why bullies harass others. They might feel the need to have power over another person or might be affected by family relationships. Sometimes bullies are on the outside of a social group looking in, and other times they are king of the hill in a group. Even the most intimidating bullies can be insecure as well.

Bullying and hazing come in many different forms, but it is all based on how the person perceives the way he or she is being treated. You may believe you are treating someone well but soon realize he or she is afraid of or intimidated by you. Sports teams often haze new members by making them complete rights of passage or withstand insults and harassment. High schools all across the world have that one kid who is always taking the nerd's lunch money. Sexual, verbal, and social harassment are also forms of bullying.

There are ways to spot victims of bullying and ways to stop it if you are that victim. All it takes is one voice standing up to a bully and witnesses will follow. If you feel like you are a victim of bullying or hazing, contact your guidance counselors, teachers, coaches, or someone you trust.

Some schools have started anti-bullying campaigns and rules against hazing. If you feel like your school isn't doing enough to reduce bullying, try talking to your principal or teachers. They can help start a chain reaction.

Top 10 Ways to Turn Down Peer Pressure

Although you don't need a reason to turn down peer pressure, here are some excuses just for fun:

1. When offered drugs, say, "No thanks, I'm already high on life."
2. Say, "My doctor says I shouldn't drink with my anti-psychotic medicine; it tends to make me crazy."
3. Say, "You wouldn't want to have sex with me; I have more STDs than a convict on death row."
4. Say, "I don't want to steal anything; this selection stinks."
5. Say, "Dude, don't make fun of them. I go play Dungeons and Dragons with them every Friday night."
6. Say, "You got anything stronger than elephant tranquilizers?"
7. Say, "Lay off my sweater man; it's sexy."
8. Spaz out and foam at the mouth.
9. Say, "What's pot? I don't want to go planting."
10. Pull an ADD moment and just walk away.

Avoiding Pressure

Though encountering peer pressure is virtually inevitable, there are ways of avoiding some situations. Look for warning signs: a party that has no supervision, a group of suspicious kids, and any other red flags such as something that you are uncomfortable just witnessing.

Knowing what to say once you are in a pressured situation is vital to everyday life as a teenager. Sometimes it is best just to tell your friends flat out that you don't want to be a part of something that may be going on. Try to make it come across as friendly and not offensive. Remember that you cannot control others' actions, but only those of yourself. However, you can suggest alternate activities in an attempt to steer your friends away from trouble.

Making excuses is probably the second most common way of avoiding pressure. This method is doomed to fail eventually, though, because at some point your friends will see through your lies. Ignoring your friends or peers who might be pressuring you is a method that may cause you to lose your friendships or relationships.

> "If you're firm and sincere about what you believe in, people will be less likely to try to pressure you."
>
> *Mrs. Burnette,*
> *English Teacher*

Watching out for potentially dangerous pressuring situations is important. It is probably even more important that you remind yourself not to make someone else the object of your own pressure. Pressuring a friend can be damaging and sometimes fatal to a relationship. True friends are aware of the kinds of situations their friends are getting into. Watch out for them, and if you are truly their friend, you won't watch them drown in something harmful. Use your best judgment, and you will probably avoid any harmful situations.

21 Ways to Say NO

LANGUAGE	HOW TO SAY "NO"
Albanian	Jo
Asturian	Non/Nun
Azerbaijani	Yox
Bahasa Malaysia	Tidak
Ellinika	O'hi
Eurish	Ara
Euskara	Ez
German	Nein
Hawaiian	A'ole
Hindi	Nahi
Irish	Ni hea/Nil
Mandarin	Bu shi
Mazahua	Pcokh
Polish	Nie
Sesotho	Tjhee
Swahili	Hapana

LANGUAGE	HOW TO SAY "NO"
Thai	Mai-chai/Mai-oua
Tieng Viet Vietnamese	Khong
Tswana	Nnyaa
Walof	Deedeet
Yiddish	Neyn

Need More Info?

Canfield, Jack, Victor Hansen, and Kimberly Kirberger, et al. *Chicken Soup for the Teenage Soul on Tough Stuff.* This source has different types of stories about difficult lessons. Sections on drugs and alcohol reflect on how negative peer pressure can affect a person's life. Stories describe teenagers who take one cigarette to fit in and then find their lives beginning to fall apart.

Hooah for Health. 7 Oct. 2004 <http://www.hooah4health. com/4life/hooah4teens/default.htm>. *Hooah for Teens* is a section of this Army website for freshmen who are feeling pressured. The teen section focuses on drugs and alcohol, tobacco and smoking, and peer pressure. Information on negative and positive peer pressure, ways to say "no," and facts about drugs and their consequences are included. There are also pages for parents and the entire family.

Kaplan, Leslie. *Coping With Peer Pressure.* New York: Rosen, 1999. This source offers an in-depth look at drug, alcohol, tobacco, sexual, gang, cult, and dating peer pressure. Coping with Peer Pressure includes chapters on avoiding peer pressure, accepting responsibility for your own actions, and moving beyond mistakes. This book offers realistic peer pressure situations that affect teens daily.

Teen Sexual Health. National Library of Medicine. 6 Oct. 2004 <www.nlm.nih.gov/medlineplus/teensexual health.html>. This site offers statistics, newsletters, and reports published in national studies. A medical site for sexually active teens, it has a section devoted to coping with sexual pressure, a glossary of terms and directories, a section regarding diagnosis and symptoms of STDs, and links to other related issues such as teen pregnancy and development during puberty.

6
Friends

More Than Just a TV Show

"The only way to have a friend
is to be one."

-Ralph Waldo Emerson

Friend (frĕnd) n.
1. A person whom one knows, likes, and trusts
2. A person with whom one is allied in a struggle or cause; comrade
3. One who supports, sympathizes with, or patronizes a group
4. An acquaintance

—www.dictionary.com

Friends

All life's experiences are more fun if shared with a friend. Coffee tastes better when shared with a friend; a walk is shorter when shared with a friend. Chocolate cake even has fewer calories when shared with a friend. True friends who are open-minded, trustworthy,  and thoughtful are a rare find, and finding a friend with these characteristics may be a difficult process. Once found, the friend should be cherished and protected like a prized possession.

"True friendship is seen through the heart, not through the eyes." These powerful words by an anonymous author apply well to every friendship. Appearance, race, gender, and age are not traits on which to base friendship. Friendship should instead be based on the characteristics that matter the

> **"Friendship is the only cement that will ever hold the world together."**
>
> *Woodrow Wilson*

most, like shared interests, genuine personality traits, and similar values. People who judge others based on appearance rather than on internal qualities may not make the best choices in friends because appearances can be deceiving. Get to know everyone regardless of what they look like, and you will be amazed at how many friends you will make. Remember, true friends are open-minded, trustworthy, and thoughtful.

Top 10 Things to Do With Friends

1. Go on a road trip.
2. See a concert.
3. Go to the movies.
4. Have a sleepover party.
5. Go shopping.
6. Have a scary movie marathon.
7. Go out to eat somewhere fancy and dress up.
8. Work out or exercise together.
9. Have Monday Night Football parties complete with your favorite snacks and beverages.
10. Dress up in your school colors and go to every sporting event for your school.

New Kids on the Block

Starting high school can be difficult; however, think of what it would be like if you moved to a new place your freshman year and had to leave all your good friends behind. Older students in particular are affected by moving. It's hard when kids have to move to a new place and leave behind the old friends who provided comfort and support. Moving can be a difficult event in a person's life, and moving into a new high school can make adjusting even more difficult.

Finding yourself in a new school is challenging, and the first week is probably the hardest. Once the school day becomes a routine and you begin talking to more people and making new friends, the day becomes much more enjoyable. It may take some

> **"The hardest thing about being a freshman is not being with friends from middle school."**
>
> *Corey, freshman*

time, but gradually you will become accepted into your new school.

A survey on smartgirl.org asked the question, "What would you do if you saw a new kid at school that people thought was different?" Sixteen percent responded saying that they would put themselves in the new kid's shoes and talk to him. Twenty-one percent said they would make friends with the new kid and tell their friends to make friends with him too. Twenty-eight percent said that peer pressure is something that you have to deal with; be stronger than it and do what you think is right. Only one percent said, "Do what your friends do, and that way you won't embarrass yourself."

So if you're the new kid, never fear. Most kids are decent enough to come up and start a conversation with you. It's only that one percent that you have to worry about.

People have different ways of meeting friends. "Try and talk to people, see what people in the area [do], what interests people [have]," advises Danny from teenwire.com. It's always good to become involved. Try out for a team or join a club. Doing so will boost your confidence and your self-esteem, and it will help you meet more people. Once you make a few friends, it's surprising how much more fun school becomes. Suddenly you have people you can talk to about homework and can hang out with on the weekends.

Top 10 Places to Meet Friends

1. At school
2. Through extracurricular activities
3. Through other friends
4. At summer camp
5. On vacations
6. At movies
7. Through siblings/cousins
8. At parties
9. At work
10. At the community pool

One's Silver and the Other's Gold

Many people think that a best friend is the person you knew when you were five and still hang around with when you are fifty. However, everyone matures and changes at different rates. Your views start to change, and then suddenly the five-year-old you grew up with is a completely different person.

Going to high school causes many teenagers to transform because they feel they have to fit into a new

> "Lots of people want to ride with you in the limo, but what you want is someone who will take the bus with you when the limo breaks down."
>
> *Oprah Winfrey*

environment. Some kids go as far as making a whole new set of friends or dressing in a completely different way. In some cases, changing friends can mean you're growing up and becoming a new person. Friendship is valuable no matter how old you are. If you feel the need to change friends, just remember that making new friends is great, but keeping the old ones whom you shared a part of your life with is priceless.

Poll

Do you have the same friends as in middle school?*

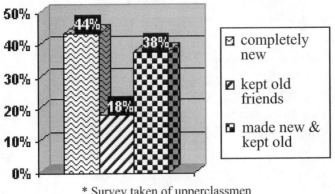

* Survey taken of upperclassmen

What kind of ships last the longest? FRIENDSHIPS!

"It was my last week in the Carolinas and I was going to miss my friends terribly. They had planned a surprise going-away party for me, which of course I knew about. I got to my friend's house to 'spend the night,' and seven of my best friends were in the backyard holding a banner that said: **'We'll miss you Maggie!'**

Then we went inside and they brought out a cake, but they dropped it! I started crying, and my friends thought it was because they dropped the cake, but it was because I realized what true friends I had."

—Maggie

"My friends and I were hanging out one day. I had known them for a long time, and we were all super close. Another kid had been hanging around us for a while, and I wasn't sure I liked him. Sure enough, he started talking bad about me. I was truly afraid that my buddies would join in on the slam fest, but instead they decided to ditch that guy. I realized then that my friends would stay true to me to the end!"

—Craig

"I was walking with my best friend in the hall one day, and sure enough I saw the cutest boy I had ever seen in my life! I was so distracted that I forgot where I was going and ran smack into an open locker! My nose started gushing blood! The guy looked at me like I was the most disgusting thing on the face of the planet. I was on the verge of tears, but luckily my friend quickly steered me to the nurse's office and even missed drama, her favorite class, to stay with me and make me feel better."

—Stecky

Top 10 Nice Things to Do for a Friend

1. Tape his favorite show or sports team's game for him.
2. Watch her sporting events.
3. Help him with homework.
4. Give her random "just because" presents/cards.
5. Bring him balloons on his birthday.
6. When she is absent from school, give her the homework assignments.
7. Bring him soup when he's sick.
8. Tell her you like her new haircut or new outfit.
9. Pay for his movie ticket.
10. If someone is making fun of her, stick up for her.

Mirror, Mirror on the Wall

Shakespeare once said, "All the world's a stage and all the men and women merely players." The quote describes how most of us in this world are just trying to play a part. But does it relate to friendships?

Everyone wants to fit in somewhere. People tend to think they need to pretend to be someone they're not to gain a friendship, not knowing that true friendships are based on genuine traits. Forcing yourself to behave in a certain way in order to impress someone else will only make you miserable. Wouldn't it be more fulfilling to have friends who are willing to accept who you really are than friends who are only accepting when you change your personality?

Eventually, wearing a lifestyle mask 24/7 will wear you out. Find friends who will appreciate who you are underneath. Those who will hang out with you only if you conform to their standards are not worth your time; don't give them the satisfaction of having control over who you are. The most important thing is always to stay true to yourself because you are your own best friend for life.

Top 10 Ways to Lose Friends

1. Tell your friend, while shopping, that the outfit she has tried on looks bad on her, and then go back the next day and buy the exact same outfit.
2. Shave off his eyebrows.
3. Call her frequently, especially in the morning, asking for Ben. No worries if you don't know a Ben. Ask for him anyway.
4. Start calling him by a horrific nickname, such as his name with an added "Poo" or something that relates to him in no way at all.

5. On Halloween, dress up as your friend saying, "Do you like my costume? It's the ugliest one I could find."

6. If your friend is running for a class office, ask her for a button. Wear it proudly on your shirt (after drawing devil horns and a mustache on it, that is).

7. After spending the night at his house one night, grab his baby blanket or cherished stuffed animal. At school the next day hold it up in the hall and scream, "Look! I found Mr. Snuffles. I knew you'd be lost without him, so I brought him as soon as I could!"

8. Call her crush and tell him your friend thinks he's a hunk-a-hunk-a-burnin-love!

9. Play the copycat game with him and repeat everything he says for hours at a time.

10. Make her a cake for her birthday, and when you hand it to her, have someone else's name all over the front. When she looks at you and says, "Uhh...that's not my name," say, "And your point is?"

Need More Info?

Carlson, Richard, Ph. D. *Don't Sweat the Small Stuff for Teens: Simple Ways to Keep Your Cool in Stressful Times*. New York: Carlson, 2000. This is a great book for finding solutions to problems in a friendship or simply any information on friendships. It talks about ways to make up after a fight and even ways to prevent a fight from happening. This book also discusses subjects like how to be a good friend, how to make a good friend, and also how to "keep your cool" in tricky situations.

Carnegie, Dale. *How to Win Friends and Influence People.* Rev. Ed. New York: Simon, 1981. This famous work offers suggestions on how to improve the reader's social life in various areas. Carnegie effectively explains how to make friends quickly, be an effective leader, and increase popularity and involvement in conversation. Though this book was not written specifically for teenagers, the principles presented in the book can improve the social life of any interested, devoted reader.

"Friends." *Cool Nurse Home Page.* 3 Oct. 2004 <http://www.coolnurse.com/friends.htm>. This article tells of the value of a group of friends and how they often become like a family because you spend so much time together. It expresses the importance of sharing certain feelings, thoughts, opinions, etc. Friendships, especially those that begin in high school, can come and go very quickly. This article explains how important it is to try and preserve them the best you can.

"Friendship is Important to Teens." *Family Works: Strategies for Building Stronger Families.* 7 Oct. 2004 <http://www.urbanext.uiuc.edu/familyworks /teen-05.html>. Friends could very well be the biggest aspect in a teen's life. This article tells how a teen with no friends tends to be more introverted and less successful throughout life. For this reason, it also gives advice on how to make friends. The majority of this article is geared towards teenagers, but at the end it focuses on the parenting side of things.

Meyer, Stephanie H., and John Meyer. "Friends." *Teen Ink: Our Voices, Our Visions*. Deerfield Beach: Health, 2-36. These friendship stories are both informative and interesting to read. In the stories, teens tell everything from how they make friends to how to deal with a friend's death. The writers come from all different backgrounds, and each writes about his or her experience. Each story ends with a great lesson learned.

Peterson, Joanne, et al. "On Friendship." *Chicken Soup for the Kid's Soul*. Eds. Jack Canfield, et al. New York: Scholastic, 1998. 33-68. Hollywood Stars contribute personal experiences and fictional stories to this collection. Average friendships are related to extraordinary stories such as a boy's escape from death as he dangled over a pit. A cornucopia of moving works from notable artists and poets encourages teens to deepen friendships and be more understanding.

Telesco, Patricia. "Moving Blues." *Teenwire Home Page*. 27 February 2004. Planned Pregnancy Federation of America. 5 Oct. 2004 <http://www.teenwire. com>. The article entitled "Moving Blues" is helpful because it offers reassurance through the moving process and explains how to be "the new kid." Telesco's article includes tips on moving from people who have been through it. One list gives tips on starting conversations and making friends after you move.

Yager, Jan, Ph.D. *When Friendship Hurts: How to Deal with Friends who Betray, Abandon, or Wound You.* New York: Yager, 2002. This is a great book for information on dealing with and solving fights between friends. It talks about why friends hurt each other and how to deal with the hurt. It also gives reasons to explain why a friend might be hurting you.

Dating

Movies, Dinners, and Meeting Their Parents...Yikes!

"The course of true love never did run smooth."

-*William Shakespeare*

Perhaps one of the greatest pressures that high school students face today is dating. Some people feel that having a steady boyfriend or girlfriend is necessary to enrich their high school experience. However, others deem being single as easier and more beneficial to a high school career. The truth is that dating has both positive and negative aspects.

The Good . . .

There are many good outcomes of having a relationship. Dating allows you to learn about the type of person you enjoy spending time with. A significant other is someone you can count on and have fun with. Also, knowing that someone cares for you and will always support you is a comforting feeling.

A boyfriend or girlfriend can easily turn a bad day around. It's great to have somebody to whom you can express your thoughts and feelings.

. . . **The Bad** . . .

The majority of high school students may not have a serious girlfriend or boyfriend. In fact, some students choose not to date in high school because there are more benefits that come with being a single, independent teenager.

Because of the time a serious relationship consumes, it can be hard to take advantage of high school's special opportunities. Extracurricular activities like clubs, sports, and fine arts are a great way to spend time productively and to make friends.

. . . **The Ugly**

Teenage couples break up every day. Although there are exceptions, most high school relationships only last about a month. A break up with someone that you feel strongly about can make you feel as though your heart has been ripped out and stomped on. At the moment, breaking up feels sad and horrible, but it also brings forth new possibilities.

Keep in mind that breaking up isn't just an ending but also a new beginning. Remember the possibility of new relationships and adventures with new friends that your old boyfriend or girlfriend may not have gotten along with. After your past relationship, you may find a new one that is more suitable to you in the long run. If and when someone breaks up with you, be optimistic about it. Bounce back from it. Get out and do something. Go see a funny movie. You may have felt like you were in love, but for most teens, love doesn't last.

Cindy was understandably upset when she realized that the "date" promised to her on Friday was nothing more than a small, dried, but tasty fruit.

Top 10 Worst Ways to Break Up with Someone

1. Say, "I just want to be friends."
2. Use instant messenger or email.
3. Write "dumped" and stick it on his or her forehead.
4. Ask a close friend to do it for you.
5. Get your mom or dad to do it.
6. Engage in a serious conversation and ask, "What's your worst nightmare?" Have him explain and then say, "Oh, really? Mine's being with you for even a minute longer."
7. Put "I want to break up with you" on the scoreboard at halftime of your high school homecoming game.
8. Plan a romantic picnic complete with a cake that says, "It's over." Meet at your planned meeting spot, hand the picnic basket and a blanket to her, and say, "Have fun!" Leave immediately.
9. March up to him and say, "You are the weakest link. Goodbye!"
10. E-mail saying, "It's over. I've fallen in love with your brother."

Abusive Relationships

Dating abuse can be defined as violence or the threat of violence within a relationship. Violence is anything that causes harm towards another person, whether it is physical, mental, or verbal. If you think you are experiencing violence or abuse in a relationship, you most likely are. Don't be afraid to ask for help, and never be embarrassed.

Not all abusers seem threatening, or at least not at first. The star athlete, the prom king, and the best looking guy in class may not seem to be likely abusers, but in actuality they are just as likely as anyone else.

Dating abuse can be avoided. Know whom you are going on a date with. Go out to public areas with someone you don't know well. The first time you experience any abuse in a relationship, get out. Don't expect it to be a one-time thing. It almost never is. If someone is willing to hurt you once, he will be willing to do it again. Trust your instincts if you feel threatened and step away from the situation.

There are numerous reasons that an abuser feels the need to use violence in a relationship. It's possible that the abuser has grown up with violence in his or her home and has just become accustomed to violence. It's also possible that the person is insecure and needs a type of power over his or her significant other. Whatever the reason, there is no excuse. Abuse is abuse, and it should never be accepted or taken lightly.

Ignoring Friends

The sad but true fact is that most high school relationships fail. They come and go, but friendships can last forever. Becoming too dependent on a boyfriend or girlfriend and forgetting everyone else is a common mistake teenagers make.

Be careful when you're in a relationship. You might ignore your friends without even realizing it. When in a relationship, try to spend at least one day of the week with your friends. Also, try to hang out with your friends and your significant other at the same time. Boyfriends and girlfriends can be friends with your friends, too.

Everybody knows that when two people break up, their friends are supposed to be on duty overtime and comfort them as much as possible. However, if you ignore your friends, there will be no one left to comfort you.

> *"Forgetting friends is almost never done on purpose. During my freshman year, my friend had her first boyfriend. At first, nothing changed, but after a while, we never talked on the phone or hung out after school anymore. I confronted her a month later and told her how hurt I was that she was ignoring me. Being completely oblivious to her behavior, she apologized to me."*

The Difference Between Dating and Having a Relationship

It seems as though many teenagers assume that dating and having a romantic relationship are the same. They're actually very different because of the intensity required for each.

According to Dictionary.com, dating is defined as "[a]n engagement to go out socially with another person." When you choose to date, you are not looking for long-term commitment. You simply want to enjoy having fun with lots of different people.

On the other hand, having a relationship means being committed to the same person for a period of time. Few teenage relationships have the potential to last a lifetime simply because teenagers are young and inexperienced in adapting to other individuals' emotional needs.

Since teenagers mature at different rates, one option may fit better than the other. Some teenagers may choose to neither date nor commit to a relationship. Keep in mind that, while dating and having relationships can be fun, they certainly aren't the most important social aspects of high school. Basic friendships are the most important. Just remember to relax and have fun because you have many more years to be an adult than to enjoy the free ride as a teenager.

Top 10 Best Places to Go on a Date

1. The movie theater
2. A restaurant
3. A school football game
4. A friend's house in a big group
5. An amusement park

6. The mall
7. A park
8. The bowling alley
9. The local beach
10. The pool

Bryan started to get nervous. Maybe this mating dance wasn't such a good idea after all.

Finding and Keeping Someone to Date

Before you start dating, there are some things you should know. Be sure to know someone's good and bad qualities and learn to appreciate both before the two of you decide to advance to a serious relationship. You should feel completely comfortable with this person, and you should never feel that he or she is mistreating you.

Talk to each other; talk about families, friends, and hobbies you both enjoy. Knowing these kinds of things will give your relationship a solid foundation and an excellent start. A relationship in which people skip this "getting to know you" phase can quickly turn sour.

> **"Letting your boyfriend or girlfriend know how you feel is one of the best ways to keep your relationship strong."**
>
> *Jessica, sophomore*

Be friends with your boyfriend or girlfriend before you move up to the next level. Friendship is what makes a relationship last. Also, if you're friends before the relationship gets really serious, you know the person on a more personal level.

Communication often keeps both members of a relationship happy. Sometimes you look at a person and decide that you would never date her, not even in a million years, just because of her looks. Try talking to her and see what she has to offer. Sometimes talking to a person brings out qualities that no one else sees but you.

You should always consider that everyone has a lot more to offer than looks. Don't be shallow by basing your relationship on the appearance or athletic ability of your partner. Sure, that's what may attract you to others, but it isn't a strong foundation for a healthy relationship.

Most importantly, trust yourself before others. If something in your mind or body is telling you that what you are doing isn't right, don't do it.

Need More Info?

Bartel, Blaine. *Every Teenager's Little Black Book on Sex and Dating*. Tulsa: Harris House, 2002. This Christian sex and dating guide touches on many topics to aid teens interested in high school relationships. This book encourages those dating to look for deeper traits in their partners. It includes what leads to a failing relationship and how to make a relationship truly work.

"First Dates." *Links 2 Love*. 2004. 12 Oct. 2004 <www. links2love.com/dating_first_date.htm>.This website is a guide to a fun first date. It talks about where to go, what to wear, and how to act on your first date. There is also a list of conversation starters and proper manners for your first date. One section reveals how to make the date comfortable.

"Keep Dates Safe." *Our Hutch-mid-Kansas Community Information Center*. 2002. 14 Oct. 2004 <http://www. ourhutch.com/teenscene/datingtips.html>.This is a website that gives you safe dating tips. Though it emphasizes that you always listen to yourself before you listen to others, the main point is helping to make sure you stay out of trouble. Though this website is more girl-geared, guys can get useful information as well.

Rabens, Susan. *The Complete Idiot's Guide to Dating for Teens*. Indianapolis: Macmillian, 2001. This book helps you with all aspects of dating, from asking someone on a date, to rejecting a date, and even to determining where your relationship is headed. It includes hints about what to do and not to do on a date.

"Teen Dating Violence." *Cool Nurse*. 2004. 14 Oct. 2004 <http://coolnurse.com/dating_violence.htm>. This site gives information about teen dating violence. It defines what dating violence is, how to prevent it, and how to get out of a violent relationship. The site includes statistics about teens in violent relationships and a list of hotlines to call.

Embarrassing
Moments

Oops! I Meant to Do That!

"The worst was when I fell into a pot of scalding cheese."

-Anonymous

Fingers are pointed at you. Your heart beats faster as your face glistens red. You feel humiliated as if the whole world is laughing at you. On the edge of emotion, you want to run away and hide at the same time. Sound familiar?

Avoiding Embarrassment

Embarrassing moments—we all have them. It's nearly impossible to avoid such situations; however, there are certain things that you can do to decrease your chances of being embarrassed. Clumsy feet, carelessness, and lack of attention are all common factors that result in embarrassment. By remaining alert and knowing your surroundings, you can take the necessary measures to avoid these circumstances. Fortunately, there are good ways to deal with situations that cannot be avoided.

How to Survive and Recover from an Embarrassing Moment

Surviving embarrassment can be difficult, but it is possible. When you feel humiliated, it's important to forget what happened and move on with your life. Even though you may recall an embarrassing experience, everyone else is likely to forget within a week.

After a while, you may look back on an incident and say to yourself, "Man that was stupid," or "I am such an idiot!" Dwelling on a situation is never a good idea. It will only make you feel bad about yourself and will lower your self-confidence. Putting yourself down can cause depression. It's destructive to bottle up your feelings, so let them out in a positive way. Express yourself in a constructive fashion. Be creative: Dance, go for a jog, or do something that you love to do!

Laughing at yourself is another effective coping method. Giggle and make the best of it. Laughter takes your mind off the seriousness of the situation. Others may mock and laugh at you, but if you know how to laugh along with them, handling the situation will prove much easier. Try not to let embarrassing moments ruin your day. If you don't act like it's a big deal, neither will anyone else. Remember, we all have our moments; don't let them get the best of you.

Embarrassing Moment Stories

It's a Small World

"So, my friends and I were at Six Flags, and we were having fun just waving and flirting with a bunch of random guys. There was one group, though, that wouldn't leave us alone. They kept following us, but I guess we couldn't blame them because we did keep teasing them. So, after we had made complete fools of ourselves by acting like we were boy-crazy zombies, one of them looked at me and said, 'Oh my gosh! Libby! Do you remember me? We used to go to school together in Michigan!' My mouth fell wide open, and I didn't know what to do for the rest of the night. It looks like he got a new impression of me."

-Libby, freshman

Best advice for this situation... Tell him you were kidding and were having fun with your girlfriends. Explain to him that you don't really act like that. Laughing it off is the best tactic to help this situation.

Color Guard

"My freshman year I was on the color guard at my high school. We all decided that the night before a particular competition we would spend the night at the school. That way, we would not have to get up so early the next morning. We had a great time eating junk food and watching movies, but eventually we were all ready to shower and go to sleep. So, we headed down to the locker room to shower. I thought that no one else would be crazy enough to be in the building that late, so after my shower, I walked out of the locker room and into the gym with just a sports bra and a towel on. Just then, the entire football team walked into the gym! I immediately bolted back into the locker room. I was so embarrassed."

-Carli, sophomore

Best advice for this situation…Pray nobody saw you and deny it if anyone mentions anything.

Don't You Hate the Cheap Stuff?

"I was in third grade, and I was talking to my friend who was wearing a black dress. Thinking that the salad dressing wasn't coming out, I kept squeezing it. I looked up and saw that there was a hole in the bag, and the salad dressing had indeed come out. It had squirted all over my friend!"

-Becky, sophomore

Best advice for this situation… Help her clean up her dress as much as possible and apologize excessively.

Poll

Which person is most embarrassing to mess up in front of?

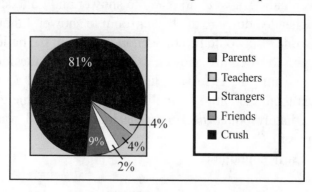

Parents: 9%
Teachers: 4%
Strangers: 2%
Friends: 4%
Crush: 81%

Capri-Sun Slip

"On the first day of my freshman year, I was walking through the junior/senior cafeteria where no freshmen normally walk. On this particular day, I was in a hurry. Not paying attention to where I was walking, I slipped on something on the cafeteria floor. I had slipped on a Capri-sun! Seconds later I was on my butt with the cafeteria food strung in my hair. The entire cafeteria burst out laughing, and all the seniors were making fun of me! I was so embarrassed."

-Kellie, freshman

Best advice for this situation…If other people are laughing at you, just laugh with them. People admire others who are able to laugh at their mistakes. Take a five-hour shower and wash your hair, too!

Things in Motion Stay in Motion...

"I had been having a pretty rotten day, and I knew chemistry wouldn't make it any better. I escaped to the bathroom. When I was exiting my stall, I gave it a kick. The door hit the wall and flung back at me. For some reason, someone decided it would be a good idea to put the hook that you find on the back of all stall doors at eye level. So, the hook banged against my head and knocked me to the ground. I gave a yelp and went back to class with every person in the hall having heard my cries of pain, looking at me like I was nuts."

-Mimi, junior

Best advice for this situation… Tell anyone that is staring at you that you got hit in the eye and it really hurts, or just ignore them.

Bathroom Floor

"It was the last day of school before Christmas break, and I found myself locked in the bathroom stall. I desperately wanted to get out and get on home. I ended up having to crawl under the door, and of course, the floor was wet with who knows what. To make matters worse, a large congregation of girls had gathered around the stall staring."

-Jorjeta, sophomore

Best advice for this situation… There isn't much you can do in this situation. Just walk away with as much dignity as you can.

Poll

How often do you do something embarrassing?

Every minute: 12%
A couple times a day: 18%
A few times a week: 35%
Not too often: 10%
Once in a blue moon: 25%

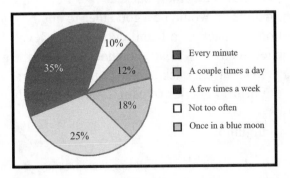

Smelly Shoes

"It was my girlfriend Linda's party for her sorority, and in my day, we had sororities in high school. She was an officer for her sorority, and I had to dress up really nice. I rented a tux with the tails and a big top hat, and I went to pick her up at her house. Linda's family had just gotten new carpet, so the house looked nice. When I got there, her father told me I looked rather sharp. As I was sitting there waiting for her to come down, I started smelling something foul. I looked around thinking that perhaps it was the old carpet, which was sitting on the lawn, but sure enough, I had stepped in some dog mess and had tracked it all over the new carpet. Her mom came down and started crying at the sight of it. What was supposed to be a memorable night just turned out to be a nightmare."

-Mr. Cooper, substitute teacher

Best advice for this situation… Help the mom clean up the mess and hope the night will turn out to be a funny memory.

The Wet Stairs

"On a rainy day at school, my friend and I were walking to a class. On our way, we saw a freshman girl walking down the stairs carrying a large stack of books and wearing sandals. The stairs were very slippery because of the rain. The girl slipped on a wet spot on the floor and dropped her books everywhere. We laughed a little, but we also felt bad for her, so we helped her pick up her books."

-Bryce, senior

Best advice for this situation…Luckily for the freshman girl, others were kind enough to help her even after her embarrassing moment. The best thing to do is to just smile, thank people for their help, and continue on as if nothing happened.

Why Do I Let Her Go Places without Me?

"My mom went shopping for me one day at some of the stores we usually go to. Too bad she didn't know which sections were for me. A shirt she thought was "totally cool" ended up being a maternity shirt, and she showed it off to me while my brother's hot friends were in the room. David (the hottest of them all) looked at it with a raised eyebrow and said, "Well, Kailie, who's the daddy?"

-Kailie, sophomore

Best advice for this situation… Say it's his kid and that you want child support.

The White Dress

"On the first day of school, I wore a white dress. While carrying my lunch from the line to the table with my friends, I tripped over my own feet and spilled chocolate milk all over my dress. I had to walk around school for the rest of the day wearing a white dress with a big, brown spot down the front. Everyone stared at me the entire day!"

-Lauren, sophomore

Best advice for this situation…If you're dealing with stained clothing, see if the cafeteria ladies or janitors have club soda or another substance to take the stain out.

Cell Phone Slip-up

"My technology class is the most boring class ever. Every day we take notes and listen to long, useless lectures. One day, to avoid the daily routine, I prepared myself for the class by sneaking in my cell phone to play games. I had been able to sneak my phone in class many times in the past, but on this day, I made a small mistake. I

had forgotten to turn my cell phone on silent mode. When I won the game, the phone started going off! The entire class looked at me in awe, and the teacher just quietly walked over to my desk, took my phone, and told me to see her after class. I looked around at all my classmates laughing at me. My face turned so red! I sank down in my desk, pretending to disappear, and I didn't say another word the entire day. Ever since that day, I have NEVER brought my phone to class!"

-Michael, sophomore

Best advice for this situation...It is probably a good idea not to bring your cell phone to any class, or make sure that you keep it on silent.

Top 10 Recoveries for Embarrassing Moments

1. If you're ever caught sleeping in class and your teacher comes and taps you on the shoulder to wake you up, say, "Amen," and look annoyed.
2. If you drop your food, say, "I didn't want it anyway."
3. If you fall down the stairs, take a bow and say, "Thank you."
4. If you fall down and scrape your knee, say, "I didn't need that leg anyway."
5. If you have food on your face, tell everyone you were saving it for later.
6. If you have a hole in your sock, tell everyone that it is an air vent.
7. If you're a freshman and you get stuffed in a trashcan, tell everyone that you're looking for your pencil.
8. If you're in church and your cell phone rings, tell everyone that God is calling you.
9. If you spill ketchup on your shirt, say that red is in this season.
10. If you get sent to the principal's office, tell him that the voices in your head made you do it.

Need More Info?

"The Ability to Laugh at Ourselves Can Be Healthy." 11 Oct. 2004 <http://humordoctormd.homestead. com /LaughOurselves.html>. This website emphasizes the importance of laughing at yourself when you make a mistake. There are also links to embarrassing stories, which can help you to feel better about your own situation.

"Embarrassing Moments: Oops!" 11 Oct. 2004 <http://www.pbskids.org/itsmylife/school/embarrassing/>. This website shares numerous suggestions on how to deal with embarrassment and offers puzzles and games about embarrassment. Sections such as "Oops," "How to Deal," and "Things to Remember" provide countless ways to laugh.

"Embarrassing Moments," and "Cool Comebacks." *J-14* October/November 2004: 16-17, 94-95. "Embarrassing Moments" includes stories from other people about their embarrassing situations. The "Cool Comebacks" section contains more stories and comebacks that people have used to recover from embarrassment.

"Oops! Embarrassing Moments." 11 Oct. 2004 <http://www.myjellybean.com/oops/oops.html>. This site gives advice on how to recover from a mortifying experience and includes realistic examples of uncomfortable scenarios.

"True Life Embarrassing Stories." *That's Embarrassing!!* 25 Sept. 2004 <http://www.thatsembarrassing.com/>. This website displays stories submitted by people all over the country whose embarrassing experiences provide humor.

Upperclassmen

Bow Down to Me!

"You give before you get."

-Napoleon Hill

Upperclassmen—one of the most feared specimens of high school (except, of course, for the occasional drivers' ed. and world history teacher). Upperclassmen are the fickle creatures that roam the halls of high school. Horror stories have probably reached your ears by now of the tortures the poor freshmen of the past have endured.

> **"The hardest thing about being a freshman is dealing with the SENIORS!"**
>
> *Alex, freshman*

Sadly, a handful of these tales are true, but not all upperclassmen enjoy tormenting you and your fellow freshmen. Most juniors and seniors say that the problem with freshmen is their "I know everything" attitude, but can you really be blamed? Making the transition from being the biggest and boldest kids in the school to being the lowest on the high school totem pole is tough,

> **The hardest thing about being a freshman is being treated like scum by the upperclassmen."**
>
> *Cherise, freshman*

and some freshmen do not know how to swallow their pride and step back. You should understand, though, that if you treat upperclassmen with genuine kindness and respect, they will not lay a finger on you.

Starting high school is nerve-racking enough with all the new surroundings; in addition, all upperclassmen seem to be a few hundred feet taller than you. Keep in mind, though, that you will be an upperclassman after your freshman year. Seniority gets better and better year after year until you're the big man on top. When senior year comes, you will be first priority and will become part of the most respected group of the school. Until that day, deal with upperclassmen the best you can; everyone else once had to also.

Dealing with Upperclassmen

So, just how does one avoid and deal with a frightening confrontation with one of these "creatures"? Don't avoid an encounter with an upperclassman as if he were the Black Plague. This idea is very foolish, believe it or not. If an upperclassman insults you, makes fun of you, or embarrasses you in front of the whole student body, its faculty, administration, custodians, and a guy named Fritz, deal with it the best you can because there is no way of escaping it. High school should be a fun time in your life. Give the upperclassmen  their two seconds of fun, laugh it off, and then go on with life. An upperclassman won't pick on you if he thinks it's not bothering you. One thing that we do not recommend is making rude jokes or comments about upperclassmen to their faces. Such actions will most definitely anger them and lessen their respect for you. Also, while making fun of upperclassmen may be entertaining in the beginning, it will certainly burn your bridges in the long run and cause friction between both parties.

> » Don't annoy upperclassmen.
> » Don't believe everything upperclassmen say.

Another way to survive the senior harassment is to mind your own business. If an upperclassman makes an embarrassing comment to you, do not respond. Keep on your intended path of travel. Remember, retaliation is not the answer (unless you come up with something really clever—then, by all means, baffle them). Some upperclassmen can be dreadful bullies and would rather beat you up than look at you twice.

As a last resort, if you are in a position to escape (ex. a crowded hallway where you can "disappear") and a situation is too intimidating, escape into the crowd by trailing one of the common and numerous "nerds" running throughout the school. ("Nerds" are the ones carrying their books out in front of them, versus on the hip, and dodging and weaving between people to surpass the average rate of speed in the hallway.) If you are not in a position to escape (ex. the upperclassman is in your math class), buckle down and ignore him. If he's not smart enough

> **"The hardest thing about being a freshman is how the seniors cut in front of us in the lunch line and we never have time to eat our food when we finally get it."**
>
> *Kelly, freshman*

to be in a class for his own grade level, he does not deserve a place in the "I really hate this person and I'm going to stew all day because of the comment he made to me this morning" section of your brain. He's not worth it. Forget about it.

> **"Don't talk to older kids."**
>
> *Merideth, senior*

Please note that the suggestions above are exactly those: suggestions. They are to be used in minor situations only. If any physical or mental abuse is executed, contact a teacher or administrator immediately. Harassment and bullying are not to be taken lightly. Reporting serious abuse can also save other freshmen from the peril of senior predators.

How to Befriend the Enemy

No matter how mean they might seem, an upperclassman is still a human being. It is possible to befriend one; it just takes a bit more work to do so. An upperclassman friend is quite valuable in high school. All people need a helping hand at some point in their lives; it helps even more if that hand belongs to someone older.

Upperclassmen usually feel an air of superiority toward underclassmen because they have gone through a couple more years than the younger kids, but underneath, they really aren't much different. However, when you first meet upperclassmen, it is very important to make them feel respected even if doing so seems difficult. If you treat an upperclassman with respect, he will see you in good light. However, if you treat him like dirt, then you will never earn his respect.

After you earn an upperclassman's respect, she will begin to treat you as one of her own and not as a freshman.

> » All upperclassmen were once freshmen.
> » Upperclassmen aren't as scary as they seem.

However, some upperclassmen will never get over the fact that you are a freshman and will always treat you differently (to their loss, of course). Nevertheless, you can still be friends with most upperclassmen. It will merely be a different form of friendship—more of a "brotherly" friendship.

Oftentimes, people have trouble meeting upperclassmen. A good way to initiate contact between you and an upperclassman is through clubs and extracurricular activities. Meeting up with a variety of people with a common interest is a great way to meet, make, and keep upperclassman friends.

Freshman Harrassment

Were you harrassed or intimidated by seniors?

Yes, often - 10%
Sometimes - 19%
Rarely - 4%
Never - 67%

Club meetings and activities provide ample time for you to befriend and get to know upperclassmen.

Upperclassmen are all different. They all have mixed feelings towards freshmen. Some will be nice to you. Can't find your next class and are going to be late? The nicer upperclassmen will help you find your way, but beware of the ones who tell you your next class is located on the third floor next to the merry-go-round.

Some upperclassmen will pick on you, make fun of you, and throw food at you at lunch. Nicknames are often given to freshmen: freshie, fresh meat, stupid freshmen, and many others. Fun little nicknames like those are harmless. As you become older, you will get to call the new freshmen these harmless names as well. When the names become harsh or offensive, however, report the behavior to a school authority. No one has the right to make you feel uncomfortable or bad about yourself.

> **"Seniors really aren't as bad as you think."**
>
> *Scott, junior*

Sibling Seniority

Going into your freshman year, one of your biggest fears may be your upperclassman brother or sister. You may have heard all the stories of how freshman siblings are the main targets for upperclassmen. These stories may make you as scared as a cornered cat. However, having an upperclassman brother or sister is not nearly as bad as you may have heard. Often, having an older sibling is more of a blessing than a curse.

One positive aspect of having an elder sibling in school with you is that he or she can give you advice. That's right: your sibling has probably been though most of the problems that you will be facing, so do not be afraid to go to him or her for advice, whether it be on academics or on relationships.

On the other hand, there are also negative aspects of having an upperclassman sibling. Sometimes their friends will pick on or even torment you a bit, but remember they would not take the time if they did not care. The easiest thing to do is just to ignore the teasing or maybe even join in with the teasing. For example if your sister's boyfriend is calling you little squirt, you could call him Goliath. If your sibling's

words start to bother you, simply ask him or her to stop. If he doesn't listen, talk to your parents.

Another low would be having the same teachers your sibling had. Say your sibling was the brightest kid in class, always sucking up and loved by the teacher; now you have to live up to that reputation. Or, your sibling could have been the worst kid in class—one who failed and was always cracking jokes. Then your teacher might not like you as much because of your sibling's previous behavior. Just be sure to establish your own reputation from the start.

50 Ways to Annoy an Upperclassman

1. Throw confetti and balloons and say, "The King has returned!" every time he enters a room.
2. When she complains, sing in a Broadway musical voice, "Why don't you put on a smile?"
3. Draw anime all over his notes.
4. Steal his notes and say his girlfriend did it.
5. Tattoo (in pen) your name on her bicep as she sleeps.
6. Refer to him as "The Upperclassman" (ex: Did you hear what The Upperclassman said to me on the bus?).
7. Translate her notes into Chinese and then act surprised when she refuses to pay you for your efforts.
8. Steal one of his socks and call it "My preciousssss" for the rest of the year.
9. Get in the fetal position and rock back and forth every time you see her.
10. Memorize what page he's on in the yearbook and recite it every time you see him.
11. Bump into her in the hallway and say you didn't see her there.
12. Constantly recite advice from your parents and older siblings that have graduated.
13. Come up with a secret handshake and act offended when he doesn't know it.
14. Throw rose petals out in front of her as she walks down the hall.
15. Make fake trumpet sounds before he speaks.
16. Write an ode to her and recite it at lunch.
17. Compose him a theme song on the bagpipe.
18. Kiss her pencils for good luck.
19. Switch the material in his binders so he has history stuff in his science binder.
20. Place an Amazonian bird-eating tarantula in her bologna sandwich.

21. When you go with him to football games, cheer for the other team and act surprised when he gives you dirty looks.
22. Wave enthusiastically and scream her name anytime (if any) she acknowledges you in the hallway.
23. Dress up as a pirate and call him "matey" all day long (with continual "Arrrrrrrrr" noises).
24. Laugh like a maniac and rub your hands together every time she makes eye contact with you.
25. Send him "upside down number text messages" on your calculator every two seconds.
26. Put on a cape with "eyespots" on it and raise it to "intimidate" her anytime she gets too close.
27. Sell him on the Internet without his knowing it.
28. Cook her a hearty breakfast of bacon, eggs, and sausage during first period.
29. Carry around a tape recorder and make notes on what he does all day.
30. Write a multiple volume novel about her life story.
31. Always refer to yourself in third person.
32. Polish his shoes.
33. Entertain her with your broad variety of knock-knock jokes.
34. Start a magnet collection and show it off to him while he's frantically typing up his term paper (which is due in thirty minutes).
35. Hide in the back of her car; when she is halfway to school, pop up and say, "Hey, can we stop at that McDonald's?"
36. Run up to him and "tag" him.
37. Call her your "study buddy."
38. Walk slowly in front of him through the hallways.

39. Talk to your friends in a large blob in the middle of the hallway.
40. Invite yourself to dinner at her house.
41. Decorate his locker for his birthday even if it isn't.
42. Laugh when she tries to make fun of you.
43. Stuff string cheese into his locker.
44. Yell, "Everyone clear the hall; a senior is coming through!"
45. Randomly show up at her house for a "slumber party."
46. Follow him everywhere.
47. Invite yourself into all of his weekend plans.
48. When she looks at you, stand up and scream, "Quit looking at me!"
49. Follow him through the halls while tugging on the hem of his shirt.
50. Hold your nose when sitting near him.

Need More Info?

Dunnahoo, Terry. *How to Survive High School: A Student's Guide*. Chicago: Frankin Watts, 1994. This book gives tips on surviving high school and discusses "real life" issues. With chapters on dealing with high school life, classes, and goals, this book is sure to answer your questions about what's ahead in life. This book is a great source for any problems a teenager may face.

"High School: Small Fish Again." 2004. PBS Kids. 1995-2004. 27 Oct. 2004 <http://www.Pbskids.org/itsmylife/school/highschool/article4.html>. This site points out that you've made this transition before; you went from elementary school to middle school. You will fit in better going along with traditions that are harmless emotionally and physically. You have a better chance of meeting upperclassmen through clubs. Get involved. Having an older sibling at the same school can introduce you to upperclassmen.

"In Their Defense." 13 Sept. 2002. 29 Oct. 2004 <http://www.weaselcorner.321Webmaster.com/custom.html>. This article discusses constant cruelty toward freshmen. The author states that she herself has been mistaken for a freshman and has mistaken other upperclassmen for freshmen, so there are no apparent defining characteristics for freshmen.

This site recognizes that upperclassmen do have seniority, and there is no reason to insult them.

Martin, Patti. "Freshman Advice!!" 27 Oct. 2004 <http://www.northstar.k12.ak.us/Schools/frontpages/hut/counseling/freshmenadvice.html>. This site deals with problems for upcoming freshmen. It provides a list of tips for upcoming freshmen on such topics as meeting new people. The writer is a high school student, so some of the suggestions may apply only to the author's school.

Frequently Asked Questions

Q: Was it a hard transition between middle school and high school?

A: Surprisingly, no. Your middle school teachers typically prepare you very well for high school, so it's pretty easy. However, if you have trouble, see your guidance counselor. Your school may also offer free tutoring.

Q: Do people have more problems in high school than middle school?

A: Yes. Many people are more tempted to be "cool," and since they are older, they have more freedom of choice; so there are lots of drugs, alcohol, sex, etc. All the typical problems of today's teenagers are crammed into one large building.

Q: What should we do if we get lost?

A: Ask a teacher or fellow classmate for help or refer to a map of the school. Most schools will let you come in a few days early to plan your route before classes begin.

Q: How long do classes usually last?

A: Usually, they last from 45 minutes to an hour long. It depends on your school and your scheduling. In some schools, you meet for two hours every other day for a year or for two hours every day for half a year. Check with your school for specific schedule details.

Q: How do you try out for sports and join clubs?
A: Pay attention to the announcements. This is how most schools convey important extracurricular information to students. If in doubt, ask the front office.

Q: Is taking AP classes more stressful than taking classes on a normal level?
A: Normally it is more stressful, but it's also worth it in the long run when colleges look at your applications.

Q: Are the classes by grade or all together?
A: It depends on what class you are taking. Many academic classes are mixed, but you will find there are some with only your grade level.

Q: What other sports are there besides football and basketball?
A: There are lots more sports than just these. There is volleyball, lacrosse, golf, swim, soccer, cross country, track, wrestling, cheerleading, dance team, tennis, and many others available.

Q: Is there ISS in high school?

A: ISS (In-school Suspension) is still in most high schools along with OSS (Out-of-school Suspension) and expulsion.

Q: Are the teachers mean or nice?

A: It depends on the teachers and opinions from the students. All teachers are different. Some are horrible; some are awesome.

Q: What is the main difference between high school and middle school?

A: The amount of freedom between classes is different. Since you are older, you don't have to take the same route every day between classes. But at the same time, this requires more responsibility.

Q: If your locker is on one side of the school, and your class is on the other side, what do you do at locker break?

A: Plan to carry as many books as you can before returning to your locker. Most schools have a bell schedule that will give you enough time to stop by and grab a few books.

Q: Do you have time to take a shower in gym class before you have to leave for the next class?

A: Yes, you usually do; however, most people don't take the time to get showers.

Q: Is it hard to fit in with people?

A: It depends on the type of people that are at the school and the type of person you are. By being friendly and starting a few conversations, you might be able to make some really nice, new friends.

Q: Are there bullies?

A: Yes. There will always be bullies, but there will also be ways to deal with them and people to help you. See chapter four for more information on this topic.

Q: Can you choose your classes?

A: Usually you get a chance at the beginning of the year to decide what classes you want to take. You may not get exactly what you choose; however, usually you will.

Q: What is it like during classes?

A: It's usually about the same as middle school. You sit in a desk with your books and listen to what the teacher says. You take notes, quizzes, tests, etc. just like you do in middle school. Sometimes you will get a teacher who uses more creative methods of teaching, making the class much more enjoyable.

Q: Do people really get stuffed inside trashcans?
A: Sadly, freshmen occasionally do. Usually, however, this only happens to the freshmen who open themselves up to such harassment.

Q: What happens if you walk into the wrong classroom and you realize it in the middle of class?
A: Simply excuse yourself from the class without making a huge deal out of it. It happens to the best of us, so don't be embarrassed.

Q: What is the most important thing in high school?
A: To do the best you can and still have fun doing it!

Q: If you're new to the school, what is the best way to make friends?
A: Always be yourself. Being a little outgoing can also help. Talk to people, ask them questions, and just be friendly to everyone.

Glossary

ACT: American College Test; standardized test composed of four sections: English, math, reading, and science

AP Course: a college level class taken in high school

AP Test: a national test taken at the end of each AP Course

College Application: a form you fill out and send to colleges that you wish to enroll in

EOCT: End of Course Test: a standardized test given at the end of specific subjects

Freshman: a student in ninth grade

Homecoming: an event held once a year for students and visiting graduates; generally involves a football game, a dance, and a parade

Junior: a student in eleventh grade

Prom: a formal dance for juniors and seniors at the end of the year; often the dances are separate for separate grades

PSAT: Preliminary Scholastic Aptitude Test; given sophomore and junior year to help students prepare for the SAT

Salutatorian: person with the second highest GPA in his or her class; usually gives a speech at graduation

SAT: Scholastic Aptitude Test; college entrance standardized test composed of math, verbal, and writing sections

Senior: a student in twelfth grade

Sophomore: a student in tenth grade

Transcript: a document containing a student's GPA in his or her classes taken during high school; sent in with a college application

Valedictorian: person with the highest GPA in his or her class; usually gives a speech at graduation

Index